TOWARD AN EFFECTIVE PULPIT MINISTRY

Toward
An by George Holmes
Effective
Pulpit Ministry

GOSPEL PUBLISHING HOUSE

Springfield, Missouri

02-0610

ACKNOWLEDGMENTS

Grateful acknowledgment is extended to copyright owners
for permission to reprint copyrighted material.

Preparation of Sermons, by A. W. Blackwood. Copyright 1948, Abingdon
Press, Nashville, Tenn.

Power in Preaching, by W. E. Sangster. © 1958, The Epworth Press,
London. Published by Abingdon Press, Nashville, Tenn.

The Pastoral Calling, by Paul Clifford. © 1961, Channel Press, Great Neck,
N. Y.

Great Pulpit Masters, chapter on J. H. Jowett by Elmer Homrighausen.
Published by Fleming H. Revell, Old Tappan, N. J.

The Approach to Preaching, by W. E. Sangster. Copyright 1951, The
Epworth Press, London.

"And Preach as You Go," by Floyd Doud Shafer. Published by *Christianity
Today,* March 27, 1961.

The Knowledge of the Holy, by A. W. Tozer. © 1961, Harper and Row,
New York.

Article on Preaching, *The New Schaff-Hertzog Encyclopedia of Religious
Knowledge.* Published by Baker Book House, Grand Rapids, Mich.

The Craft of Sermon Construction, by W. E. Sangster, Copyright 1949,
The Epworth Press, London.

Letter from a reader, *Christianity Today,* December 8, 1967.

Power in Expository Preaching, by Farris D. Whitesell. © 1963 Fleming
H. Revell, Old Tappan, N. J.

We Prepare and Preach, by Clarence Stonelynn Roddy. © 1959, Moody
Press, Moody Bible Institute of Chicago.

A Professional Storywriter's Handbook, by Edwin A. Peeples. © 1960,
Doubleday & Co., New York.

Take It Easy, by W. B. Pitkin. Copyright 1935, Simon & Schuster, Inc.,
New York, and *Reader's Digest,* Pleasantville, N. Y.

Scripture quotations marked Phillips are from *The New Testament in
Modern English,* translated by J. B. Phillips. © 1958, The Macmillan Company, New York and Geoffrey Bles Ltd., London.

TOWARD AN EFFECTIVE PULPIT MINISTRY
© Copyright, 1971
by the Gospel Publishing House
Springfield, Missouri 65802

Library of Congress Catalog Card Number: 72-152056
Printed in the United States of America

to
SUSIE ELIZABETH
my
beloved wife
and
fellow laborer in the gospel
for
thirty years

FOREWORD

There is no greater calling than that of the preacher of the gospel. Possibly that is why there is no other calling which is more often the target of abuse by critics both outside and inside the church. Too often preaching is open to criticism because of weakness and carelessness due to lack of prayerful preparation for the task.

In certain quarters there is a feeling that the days of the pulpit are gone—that preaching is obsolete. If that be so, we have parted company with the New Testament.

Preaching must be given—if need be, restored to—its rightful place. "It pleased God by the foolishness of *preaching* to save them that believe." When our Lord began His ministry, He came *"preaching* the gospel." The apostle Paul, by the inspiration of the Holy Spirit, wrote to the young man Timothy, *"Preach the word."*

All through history God's great men have been preachers, Noah was a preacher! Moses was a preacher!

7

The prophets from Elijah to Malachi were preachers! John the Baptist was a preacher! Our Lord was a preacher! The apostles were preachers! And the Bible says, "How shall they hear without a preacher?"

Preaching has always been the minister's greatest opportunity and responsibility. History shows that preaching is the barometer of the Church. Christianity, in a sense, stands or falls with its preaching. When preaching has been dynamic, the Church has been strong; when preaching has been insipid, the Church has been weak.

Dr. R. C. Campbell says there are two kinds of preachers; one who has to find something to say and the other who has something that must be said.

George Holmes has, in this book, devoted himself to challenging preachers to preach. As the title implies, this is a book written to help men prepare for preaching. It is well-written, interesting, easy-to-read, practical. The author quotes widely and uses what he has gathered in an effective manner to spice his own material.

I have found these chapters to be personally helpful. The author has rendered the preacher a valuable service. Dealing in technique, he is not lost in it; he knows there is something beyond technique. The book will be a welcome addition to the library of the student preparing for the ministry, to the young minister undertaking his first charge, and to the minister of experience who is reevaluating his own preaching.

It is my conviction that no other activity can adequately take the place of effective, scriptural, Spirit-anointed preaching.

G. RAYMOND CARLSON

PREFACE

A book dealing with car racing does not cover all aspects of the automobile. Likewise, this book does not touch upon all the work of a minister. It focuses upon what is perhaps his most crucial task—his ministry in the pulpit.

It is written with the beginner in mind. A. W. Blackwood, from his great teaching experience, points out that "at the seminary a student may pass a number of courses but never really master homiletics and public speaking and out in the parish he may continue to flounder as a preacher."* This, surely is a sad state and one that needs rectifying. Perhaps too many young men hope there is some magic formula or a single dynamic sentence that—if they can find it—will enable them to produce breathtaking sermons instantly.

Fortunately, this is not so. The ministry is the highest of professions. It is also the hardest work

---

*A. W. Blackwood, *Preparation of Sermons* (Nashville, Tenn.: Abingdon Press, 1948).

there is. Its rewards are the greatest, but its disciplines are the most demanding. The combination of all that is required cannot be learned except through arduous, long practice and study.

This book, therefore, restates, illustrates, and honors many ancient and basic truths. It is not clever to degrade the past, and it ill becomes us to do so. Who today is producing lines comparable to Shakespeare's? in spite of dictating machines, typewriters, and computers. Think of the labor of such a man, writing with a quill pen and possibly by the light of a candle. Consider the amount and quality of his output; it will balance your perspectives.

The beginner preacher is first in view. But the author hopes that the more experienced minister will find stimulation and even, perhaps, a kick in the shins.

The book has been written, revised, typed, and retyped in homes and motels while the author has been ministering in churches, colleges, and seminars. It has been a joy to produce and it is sent forth with the prayer that God will use it to help and encourage preachers.

GEORGE HOLMES

CONTENTS

Mission

No wonder then that God made His only Son a preacher, that the first thing we are told of Jesus actually doing in the oldest of our gospels is "Jesus came into Galilee preaching"; that when Jesus commissioned the Twelve He sent them forth, first to preach, and then to heal. The Church has had the modern youth-club for thirty years, the cinema and Girl Guides for just over forty; Sunday schools for a little more than one hundred and seventy, and preachers for nearly 2,000.

—W. E. Sangster
Power in Preaching

1
MISSION

Preaching, some men feel, is oversold. After a few years out of seminary they compare the hours spent in preparation for the Sunday sermon with the apparent results and ask, "Is it worth it?"

The gloom deepens when it is realized that only fifty percent of the folk are in church on any given Sunday and a personal attendance of two Sundays out of four is average. "Counseling is more fruitful," sighs the discouraged man. "More training should be given for this."

"The small group," others maintain, "presents the dynamic situation. After all, preaching to a captive audience is a tradition from the old days when there was little else to entertain. Only ten percent of what the preacher says is retained anyway; so why waste hours preparing a sermon?"

"The solemn dignity of the ritual is what counts," declares another. "Worship is more than preaching." And so, a ten-minute sermonette is offered to people who are quite used to eating on the run.

It would be foolish to dismiss these statements as empty talk. Most of us have been eaten up by discouragement through lack of results. Yet our personal feelings and estimates must not be allowed to obscure this high view of preaching: "I urge you . . . as we live in the sight of God and of Christ Jesus (whose coming in power will judge the living and the dead), to preach the word of God. Never lose your sense of urgency, in season or out of season. Prove, correct and encourage, using the utmost patience in your teaching . . . stand fast in all that you are doing, meeting whatever suffering this may involve. Go on steadily preaching the Gospel and carry out to the full the commission that God gave you" (2 Timothy 4:1, 2, 5; Phillips). The preacher stands between his people and judgment at the final audit. Urgency, resolution, and a sense of commission are required of him at all times.

A minister, surely, is not called by God to fill, painlessly, twenty Sunday morning minutes with topical news and views. Face to face with the people he is to let loose the eternal Word of God, directing to conscience and will a message from the Almighty.

"It pleased God by . . . preaching . . ." (1 Corinthians 1:21.) Here is the *sovereignty of preaching*. It is *the* method chosen by God. Often in the past has He used the seemingly ridiculous. Noah's ark must have seemed a grotesque object, but it was God's means of salvation to those who reverenced His commands.

Other illustrations abound, but why do we need them when God specifically states He "has chosen what the world calls foolish to shame the wise; He has chosen what the world calls weak to shame the strong. He has chosen things of little strength and small repute, yes and even things that have no real existence to explode the pretensions of the things that are—that no man may boast in the presence of God" (1 Corinthians 1:27-29, Phillips).

Consider this from another angle. Today, the most effective medium of instruction is considered to be dramatic participation. Next come demonstrations; then still pictures with recordings; and finally, verbal symbols. Preaching, therefore, ranks lowest as a medium of instruction. But by choosing it as His method for teaching time's greatest news, God sealed it with an undeniable supremacy.

Bernard's *Faithful Shepherd* (written in 1621) gives preaching its honored and Biblical status: "Preaching is not a labor of the lips and an idle talk of the tongue from a light imagination of the mind: but is indeed an uttering of God's truth from a serious meditation of the heart, in sound judgment, acquired through God's blessing by diligent labor and study to profit God's people. This preaching is of worth, deserves esteem, procures credit to God's ordinance, will work upon the hearers, and will pierce deeply, as being spoken with authority."

Certainly, the foolishness of God is wiser than men.

"Christ sent me not to baptize, but to preach the Gospel" (1 Corinthians 1:17). Here is shown the *priority of preaching*. The implication is not that baptism is unimportant, but that preaching is foremost. "Sent . . . to preach": commission and task are both of divine origin. Firm remembrance of this holds a man to the course during his stretches of discouragement or exhaustion. By this he is anchored through emotional hurricanes and patient when doldrums becalm him. "God sent me," he affirms.

"God has a definite life-plan for every human

person, girding him visibly or invisibly for some exact thing which it will be the true significance and glory of his life to have accomplished." The young preacher should ponder his present and future plans in the light of these words of Horace Bushnell. If the ministry appears less than a *sacred* calling and preaching not the *passion* of his life, he is heading for dismal disillusionment. But if he is sure of God's commission and is dedicated to its utmost fulfillment, then let him listen to the song of Samuel Chadwick one of British Methodism's greats and founder of Cliff College:

> I have loved my job with a passionate and consuming love. I would rather preach than do anything else I know in this world. I have never missed a chance to preach. I would rather preach than eat my dinner, or have a holiday, or anything else the world can offer. I would rather pay to preach than be paid not to preach. It has its price in agony of sweat and tears, and no calling has such joy and heartbreaks, but it is a calling an archangel might covet; and I thank God that of His grace He called me into this ministry. Is there any joy like that of saving a soul from death? Any thrill like that of opening blind eyes? Any reward like the love of little children, to the second and third generation? Any treasure like the grateful love of hearts healed and comforted? I tell you, it is a glorious privilege to share the travail and the wine of God. I wish I had been a better minister, but there is nothing in God's world or worlds I would rather be.

"The preaching of the cross . . . is foolishness" (1 Corinthians 1:18). This indicates the *content of preaching*. Not only is God's chosen method apparently nonsensical, but so is His message, the Cross. In Paul's day, Greek philosophy and Jewish prejudice scorned the preaching of the Cross: it was beneath their dignity. "The Jews ask for miraculous proofs and the Greeks an intellectual panacea," said the apostle, "but all we preach is Christ crucified" (1 Corinthians 1:22, 23, Phillips). Today, both message and method seem outdated to the many that have been nurtured on evolutionary biology, scientific determinism, and nuclear physics. "We broadcast," writes R. E. O. White, "to minds tuned to other wavelengths, within an intellectual culture coming to be based upon non-Christian assumptions and expressed in non-Christian terms."

Corinth had its palaces of prostitution, its temples of sensuality, its drinking clubs and strongarm syndicates; there were people and places to help its many sailors dissipate themselves and their wages. It was a society unsurpassed in licentious living; slaves outnumbered citizens. How ridiculous to preach of love, the spirituality of God, peace, humility, and equality in such a society; how contrary to its philosophy and morals. "You may as well know now," writes Paul, looking back on his arrival in Corinth, "that it was my secret determination to concentrate entirely on Jesus Christ Himself and the fact of His death upon the Cross" (1 Corinthians 2:2; Phillips).

Christ, then, is the message for all time, and so *we* must preach.

We preach Jesus Christ Himself; we preach, therefore, His eternal being and preexistence, noting His theophanic appearances to man.

We preach Jesus Christ Himself as the Incarnate Son, proclaiming the miracle of that Incarnation and the mystery of the Virgin Birth, observing the witness given to it by prophets, angels, history, and apostles.

We preach Jesus Christ Himself, showing the significance of the silent years, years of preparation. We give ourselves to the study of His two natures, divine and human, so that we can more fully appreciate and preach His atonement.

We preach Jesus Christ Himself and the relevance of His baptism, anointing, temptation, sinlessness; His unique words and works. We learn of Him and then tell of Him as He reveals the Father by His life, in His teaching, and through His miracles.

We preach Jesus Christ and Him crucified, the Saviour of the world. Reverently we study His own revelations concerning His death, the prophetic foretellings, and the witness of history. We ponder constantly the amazing facts of the Cross, the profound and far-reaching effects of it, and its searching personal application for all time.

We preach Jesus Christ Himself as risen Lord and victorious accomplisher of the mighty plan of redemption.

We preach Jesus Christ Himself, ascended to heaven and active as High Priest of His people "in the power of an endless life."

We preach Jesus Christ Himself as destined judge of the world and, at His second coming, its ruler.

We preach Christ, the power of God; loving, seeking, saving, regenerating, sanctifying, and glorifying His people.

We preach Christ, the wisdom of God. "He has become for us the true Wisdom, a matter, in practice, of being made righteous and holy, in fact, of being redeemed" (1 Corinthians 1:30, Phillips).

Here is the merest outline of the message of Jesus Christ Himself. We should remember, in addition, Augustine's pertinent advice and look for Jesus *latent* in the Old Testament, as we have seen Him *patent* in the New. No wonder a bright star in the world's galaxy of preachers, Charles Haddon Spurgeon, said: "If I were forbidden to enter heaven, but were permitted to select my state for all eternity, I should choose to be as I sometimes feel in preaching the Gospel."

"By . . . preaching to save them that believe": this is the great *purpose of preaching*. We preach a Person; it is that Person men are to trust; not a philosophy or facts about Him, but Himself. That which has brought God into human focus is Jesus Christ and Him crucified. *Believing,* as pointed out in the Amplified Version, means "to adhere to, cleave to; to trust, to have faith in; to rely on." Believing on Jesus Christ is *laying hold* of Him. To lay hold of one thing, you have to let go another. This letting go is repenting: a condition that must precede absolute reliance on the Lord Jesus Christ as personal Saviour. Believing, therefore, is more than an initial act: it is a continuing trust in Christ. The Christian learns to *walk* by faith."

Salvation brings forgiveness of sins: acquittal from sin's *guilt* and deliverence from its *penalty*. On its positive side it shows the way to victory over the *power* of sin and the establishing of righteousness in the life.

Salvation means justification with relation to the past, sanctification in the present and until Christ returns, and then glorification with Him. Starting, like natural life, with a miracle of quickening, it is followed by a daily sustaining miracle and will include a consummating miracle. Less than this is a caricature of the real.

Finally, we are shown the *power for preaching:* "Not with wisdom of words." The preacher has not to depend on the persuasiveness of clever words or eloquent language but may know the "demonstration of the Spirit and of power" (1 Corinthians 2:4). This means the greatest need of every preacher, essentially, is the anointing of the Holy Spirit upon his life and ministry. This is what lifts preaching to its highest realm, making it not simply a medium for conveying Christian truth but for bringing men to Christ by a personal encounter with Him.

This anointing can be known while you are involved in your study of the Word. It must be sought in a special way in the moments before you preach so that your heart will glow with passion. This unction personalizes the Living Word and so makes a Person to person presentation of Christ a reality—through the preached word.

Again, it is unction that lifts a preacher out of himself and makes people aware of a mysterious difference. It is not produced by oratory, personalities, or intellectual attainments. It seems to cling, like the fragrance of the Holy Presence, to a man who knows God in the closet of secret prayer.

To preach Christ: this is our mission.

Messenger

Therefore the abiding right to proclaim the word of Jehovah is the conviction of Divine authority. The Divine ordination and the Divine revelation of that ordination to the soul of a man; these things are necessary, if we have to preach to thousands, or talk to tens, or deal with one soul, about the word of Jehovah.

—G. Campbell Morgan
Studies in the Prophecy of Jeremiah

2

MESSENGER

What makes a man a messenger of God? Does he choose the ministry because its excitement and glamour lure him? or because he is urged on by well-meaning friends? or was caught by an impassioned appeal for recruits? Many ministers, quite evidently, are in circulation for reasons like these; but surely there must be a more authoritative cause for devoting oneself to this high and holy task. What is it?

Great men of the Bible—patriarchs, judges, prophets, and apostles—are ready with their reasons and all agree on one thing: they were called of God. Paul, declaring his own conviction (Ephesians 3:7, 8), answers our inquiry: Why does a man become a messenger of God?

He is *appointed* by God: "...I was made a minister...." Every Christian, inevitably, is a witness for his Lord. To vitalize this he may receive divine enduement. But of ministerial appointment, we affirm:

"No man taketh this honour unto himself, but he that is called of God" (Hebrews 5:4).

Before he is ordained or installed in any pastorate, a man must have wrestled with an undeniable inward constraint from God: an anguished compulsion that leaves him no alternative but to give himself completely to the work of the ministry. This must be so unavoidable and abiding that it settles into an absolute conviction. Then, no contrary arguments will be able to move it; they will only root it more firmly.

Further, no church or council can give this call, though both should recognize its evidence. Barnabas and Saul were, first, personally called by God; then, during a period of fasting and ministry, that call was confirmed to others in the church (Acts 13:1, 2).

Such direct calling and appointment are the seals of a man's God-given authority. "If it be said," declares W. E. Sangster, "that we are taking a view of preaching so high and awful that any man might well shrink from it—the inference must not be resisted. It *is* a high and awful task from which any man might well shrink. That is why the Church in her wisest hours has always insisted that a man must have a divine call to it. The work cannot be sustained on anything less." It would be fitting if ordinands were required to show evidence of and testify clearly to such a call.

Yet all this is cloaked in mystery—and rightly so. The sacredness of the perceptive moment when a man finally decides that God *has* called him will be forever enshrined in his heart. God has honored him with the highest vocation. Later, his call may be questioned; but the man who lives in God will know his life and work somehow have their origin and purpose in the eternities.

"Brethren," Spurgeon admonished his students, "don't go into the pulpit if you can keep out of it." The urge must be irresistible, the calling sure.

The minister is a *steward of God:* ". . . according to the gift of the grace of God given. . . ." As stewards we must always be mindful of our divine appointment and potential. "Through the grace of God we have different gifts. If our gift is preaching, let us preach to the limit of our vision. If it is serving others, let us concentrate on our service; if it is teaching, let us give all we have to our teaching; and if our gift be the stimulating of the faith of others let us set ourselves to it. Let the man who is called to give, give freely; let the man who wields authority think of his responsibility; and let the man who feels sympathy for his fellows act cheerfully" (Romans 12:7, 8, Phillips). Faithful development and wise use of our God-given potential is our responsibility.

If a young man has certain capacities, training and diligence may make him a scholar, philosopher or a man of letters; but a true minister will have a *charisma*—peculiarly his. No education or study can impart this; unless it is given from above it cannot be received. With the reality of it, however, comes accountability for it. In fact, in the consciousness of it the man lives and moves and has his being.

The minister is *equipped* by God, ". . . by the effectual working of his power. . . ." "That power," let us be reminded, "is the same divine energy which was demonstrated in Christ when He raised Him from the dead and gave Him the place of supreme honor in heaven—a place that is infinitely superior to any conceivable command, authority, power, or control, and which carries with it a Name far beyond any name that could ever be used in this world or the world to come" (Ephesians 1:19-21, Phillips).

Christ, as a result of His resurrection, both bestows gifts on men and gives spiritually equipped men to His Church. It is by that resurrection power, moreover, that God's stewards are enabled to fulfill their ministry to the Church. "His gifts were made that Christians might be properly equipped for their service, that the Whole Body might be built up until the time comes when, in the unity of common faith and common knowledge of the Son of God, we arrive at real maturity—that measure of development which is meant by 'the fullness of Christ'" (Ephesians 4:12, 13; Phillips). The Lord's messenger, therefore, is equipped by the One who appointed him, and the work he does has the distinction of being eternal.

He is *dependent* upon God: ". . . Unto me, who am less than the least of all saints, is this grace given. . . ." The wonder and grandeur of God's calling amazes and humbles the man of God. The commission overwhelms; the vision prostrates by its brilliance. Like rolling thunder from some cloud-draped Sinai, the awesome sound of God's word was caught by Jeremiah: "Before I formed thee in the belly I knew thee; and before thou camest forth out of the womb I sanctified thee, and I ordained thee a prophet to the nations." Stunned by the impact of this ordination and charge, Jeremiah gasps, "Ah, Lord God! behold, I cannot speak: for I am a child" (Jeremiah 1: 5, 6). The contrast between the omnipotent sweep of God's hand and the scratching of the human pencil point is staggering.

Recognition of our frailty and utter dependence on God will make us approach our task with a wholesome reverence. Shuffling familiarity with the Word and shallow preaching are to be shunned: they are incompatible with our vocation. After a few lessons from a journalism correspondence school, a delighted student gushed to his teacher: "You have taught me to write with great facility." The immediate reply was: "I hope to teach you to write with great difficulty."

Arrogant self-confidence toward the work of the ministry is a constant peril. The more we know, the better we should realize our ignorance. Distrust of self is healthy, for it will condition our soul to look up to God. "Less than the least of all saints" cuts through professional airs, stifles jealousy at birth, peals off pride, and deflates bumptiousness. It promotes truth in our inward parts, respect in the pulpit, and humility in the prayer closet. It is the secret of learning God's leading and the pathway to glory. The preacher will know true success or failure in his life's inner realm.

Further, he is *directed* by God: ". . . I should preach among the Gentiles. . . ." In the New Testament, several Greek words are translated "preaching." One of the most common means "to proclaim as a herald." Years ago in England the town crier on horseback would come clopping fussily along the cobbled high street like a minor god visiting the earth. At the clanging of his bell and rasping "Oyez, Oyez," the citizens would flock to the town square. His mightiness, elegant in braided uniform, would take a prominent stance on the stone steps of a memorial. He would unroll his parchment and clear his throat with suitable seriousness. Then ponderously savoring each syllable, his eyes roving over those lesser mortals who were hanging on his words, he would intone the official message. His departure would be equally impressive. Now, while he officially was a proclaimer, personally he might be indifferent to the news he brought. But Christ's proclaimer—the preacher—has been arrested by God and then pressed into His service. He totally believes what he proclaims. This is the genius of preaching: ". . . That . . .

which we have heard, which we have seen with our eyes, which we have looked upon, and our hands have handled, of the Word of life ... declare we unto you" (1 John 1:1, 3).

God not only gives the messenger his work, He also directs him to his sphere. It is to be hoped the Lord's representative will not hop around like an opportunist and be motivated by political strategy. If such inducements as bigger crowds, higher salary, easier living are going to be his criteria, he had better take up other work before he becomes frustrated to the point of desperation. Preferably, the calm, confident words of Madam Guyon should express his single mindedness:

> While place we seek, or place we shun,
> The soul finds happiness in none;
> But with my God to guide my way,
> 'Tis equal joy to go or stay.

He is *instructed* by God: "... *The unsearchable riches of Christ.*" What a treasury—the riches of Christ. What extravagance—the incalculable riches of Christ. In Him reposes an exhaustless wealth of mercy, grace, and love.

It is God showing you His bullion vault and saying: "Preacher, here are infinite riches. Come as often as you like; take all you need. Give it away; share it; it is inexhaustible."

It is the Almighty pointing to the limitless ocean and saying: "Preacher, try and cross those untrackable distances and plumb those fathomless depths; then tell all you have seen. Try again and again; this is infinitude; this is Christ."

Christ, the spoken Word of the Almighty; appointed Heir of all things.

Christ , the image of the invisible God; the firstborn of every creature.

Christ, the Bread of Life, the Rock of Ages, the Mighty God.

Christ, Teacher come from God; the Desire of all nations.

The unsearchable riches of Christ.

In 1829, a clergyman, Charles Bridges, wrote a comprehensive volume titled *The Christian Ministry*. Within twenty years it had gone through nine editions. The book has a section on the causes of ministerial inefficiency in relation to personal character. As preachers, we shall often exhort people to "come up to the standard," but how about ourselves? Perhaps a thoughtful reading of the following chapter headings will probe or prod us. A minister's character is even more important than his preaching. At the same time it is part of his preaching—the nonverbal part. "What you are shouts so loudly that I cannot hear what you say," has more truth in it than we like to think.

Here then, according to Bridges are causes of ministerial inefficiency:

1. *Want of entire devotedness of heart to the Christian ministry.* "Give thyself wholly to [these things] that thy profiting may appear to all. Take heed unto thyself, and unto the doctrine; continue in them; for in doing this thou shalt both save thyself and them that hear thee" (1 Timothy 4: 15, 16).

2. *Conformity to the world.* "I have given them thy word; and the world hath hated them, because they are not of the world, even as I am not of the world. I pray not that thou shouldest take them out of the world, but that thou shouldest keep them from the evil" (John 17:14, 15).

3. *The fear of man.* "God hath not given us the spirit of fear; but of power and of love, and of a sound mind. Be not thou therefore ashamed of the testimony of the Lord" (2 Timothy 1:7, 8).

4. *The want of Christian self-denial.* "If thy right eye offend thee, pluck it out, and cast it from thee" (Matthew 5:29).

5. *The spirit of covetousness.* "For loving money leads to all kinds of evil, and some men in the struggle to be rich

have lost their faith and caused themselves untold agonies of mind. But you, the man of God, keep clear of such things" (1 Timothy 6:10, 11, Phillips).

6. *Neglect of retirement.* "We will give ourselves continually to prayer, and to the ministry of the word" (Acts 6:4).

7. *The influence of spiritual pride.* "Shall the axe boast itself against him that heweth therewith? or shall the saw magnify itself against him that shaketh it?" (Isaiah 10:15).

8. *Absence or defect of personal religion.* "See that [people] look up to you because you are an example to them in your speech and behavior, in your love and faith and sincerity" (1 Timothy 4:12, Phillips).

9. *Defect of family religion and the want of connection of the minister's family with his work.* "He must have proper authority in his own household, and be able to control and command the respect of his children. (For if a man cannot rule in his own house how can he look after the Church of God?)" (1 Timothy 3:4, 5, Phillips).

10. *Want of faith.* "Not that we are sufficient of ourselves to think any thing as of ourselves; but our sufficiency is of God' (2 Corinthians 3:5).

Unexpectedly, perhaps, Ecclesiastes offers us a miniature etching of a wise preacher: "And moreover, because the preacher was wise, he still taught the people knowledge; yea, he gave good heed, and sought out, and set in order many proverbs. The preacher sought to find out acceptable words: and that which was written was upright, even words of truth. The words of the wise are as goads, and as nails fastened by the masters of assemblies, which are given from one shepherd" (Ecclesiastes 12:9-11). This picture invites our study.

HIS TASK

Teaching: "He still taught the people knowledge. . . ." To the ungodly, the wise preacher explains the way of salvation: he does the work of an evangelist.

To the Christians, the preacher teaches the way of

holiness. He is one of God's pastors that "feed . . . with knowledge and understanding" (Jeremiah 3:15). Could anything sum up *our* work more concisely?—teaching knowledge. Probably the most desperate need of the church in America today is for Christians to "continue in the faith grounded and settled" (Colossians 1:23). If we are to maintain a stedfast position in the faith, we must be rooted in the "first principles of the oracles of God". How else can we worship and serve God aright? Other than this, what armour and weapons do we have? The unlearned are the unstable: God's people can be destroyed for "lack of knowledge" (Hosea 4:6).

We shun the mechanical repeating of a creed; for many, this is the sum and substance of their religion. Yet, do we give sufficient thought to a great declaration like the Apostles' Creed? Could it not become, at least, an outline of essential knowledge that should be taught to believers?

For reference and emphasis, the Apostles' Creed is here quoted:

> I believe in God the Father Almighty,
> Maker of heaven and earth:
> And in Jesus Christ His only Son our Lord;
> Who was conceived by the Holy Ghost,
> Born of the Virgin Mary,
> Suffered under Pontius Pilate,
> Was crucified, dead, and buried;
> He descended into hell;
> The third day He rose again from the dead;
> He ascended into heaven,
> And sitteth on the right hand of God
>   the Father Almighty;
> From thence He shall come to judge
>   the quick and the dead.
> I believe in the Holy Ghost;
> The holy Catholic Church;
> The communion of saints;
> The forgiveness of sins;
> The resurrection of the body;
> And the life everlasting. Amen.

Thomas Watson, an English divine of the 17th century, made use of the Shorter Catechism of the Westminster Assembly (1643-1649) to teach his people knowledge. Because he was a Puritan, this good man, with others, drew the hatred of the establishment and was ejected. He suffered the loss of all things for Christ.

His catechetical sermons—176 in all—were so thorough that after his death they were published as a *Body of Divinity*. To read his explanatory answers to the questions in the catechism is like overhearing a faithful minister teaching his people knowledge. We yearn that such solid instruction might be more in evidence today.

For instance, the first question, so well known, is: "What is the chief end of man?" The required answer is: "Man's chief end is to glorify God and enjoy Him for ever." Watson first explains what "glorifying God" means. Second, he shows why we must glorify God and, third, how we may know when we aim at God's glory. Under this last heading he has 17 divisions. Supported by Scripture references he lays down truth that will firmly establish, spiritually strengthen, and mentally settle any flock of God.

While recognizing our different day and age, we affirm that something more deliberate and detailed is necessary than is found in the diet of the average church.

HIS STUDY

Meditation: "He pondered. . . ." This almost lost art suffers most from organizational erosion. It is ousted from the house of its friends because they haven't time for it. But does not low regard for this treasure point up our poor sense of values?

What we are convinced has first claim on our time will, in the end, take precedence over everything. If committee meetings crowd out the hours we have resolved to spend in the secret place of the Most High, then we are forced to the conclusion that, whatever we say, in our heart of hearts we believe that public engagements are more important than waiting upon God. The truth is that ministers have absorbed as much as anyone else the restlessness of the age. A premium is placed on overt activity and we have not come to terms with prayer as the highest activity in which man can engage.°

"While I was musing the fire burned: then spake I with my tongue" (Psalm 39:3). The fire fueled by meditation in the Word is genuine: the wise preacher will give his best hours to this.

Investigation: "He sought out. . . ." Gathering, noting, and shaping material for use in preaching and teaching occupies a large part of a minister's daily life. Usually, he enjoys this part of his work and pursues it diligently. He knows "the lips of the wise disperse knowledge—sifting it as chaff from the grain" (Proverbs 15:7; the Amplified Bible).

Homiletics: ". . . [he] set in order many proverbs. . . ." The preacher's convictions become crystallized: his delivery of the truth is orderly and attractive. Notice: there is variety—*many* proverbs.

HIS PREACHING

Clear: "He sought to find out acceptable words. . . ." High-sounding words may attract him; but he goes for the simpler kind, striving to make his messages understood.

Truthful: "To write down rightly words of truth or correct sentiment. . . ." (Amplified). He is not prone to fly off on speculations or pour out sentimental nonsense for the sake of applause, but keeps to the main arteries of the good Word.

Uncompromising: "The words of the wise are as goads. . . ." Because he does not disguise sin, either to sinner or saint, the wise preacher knows that at times

---

°Paul Clifford, *Pastoral Calling* (Great Neck, N. Y.: Abingdon Press, 1961).

consciences will smart. He also knows this is one of God's ways of prodding reluctant wills.

Practical: "As nails. . . ." Pointed sermon headings will make his messages stick in the mind. His people will remember his teaching.

Skillful: "Fastened by the masters of assemblies. . . ." Because he studies to master his art, the wise preacher knows what he is about. He drives home the truth, point by point and, by keeping to the point, helps his people to see the point.

HIS AUTHORITY

"Given from one shepherd . . .": that is, the Good, the Great, the Chief Shepherd. As Christ took the loaves and fishes, broke and gave them to the disciples to distribute, so the wise preacher receives his food from the Shepherd and, breaking it down, feeds it to his flock.

He sees his work against a backdrop of death, judgment, and eternity: "Or ever the silver cord be loosed, or the golden bow be broken, or the pitcher be broken at the fountain, or the wheel broken at the cistern" (Ecclesiastes 12:6). Bishop Gore, giving his final charge to candidates on the eve of their ordination, used to say: "Tomorrow, I shall say to you, wilt thou? wilt thou? wilt thou? But there will come a day when another will say to you, hast thou? hast thou? hast thou?"

In his chapter on J. H. Jowett, in *Great Pulpit Masters,* Elmer Homrighausen writes:

> All his energies, spiritual, mental, nervous and physical were concentrated on preaching and preparation for preaching. He read, observed, thought, meditated and brooded with a single eye to the pulpit; he scorned delights and lived laborious days to perfect himself for his high calling.*

He was a wise preacher; he was the messenger of God.

---

*Elmer Homrighausen, *Great Pulpit Masters* (Old Tappan, N. J.: Fleming H. Revell).

Mainspring

The word of Jehovah which is to be delivered to an age, to nations, to men, always comes to souls prepared to receive it, by acquaintance with the Secret Place. When God has need of the proclamation of His word, He must find as an instrument, one who in his own personal and private life has become familiar with the voice of God. The call is often sudden, but it is always spoken to a man who is already in the Divine secret, knowing something of the ways of God.

—G. Campbell Morgan
Studies in the Prophecy of Jeremiah

3

MAINSPRING

Lengthening shadows brought the Jewish Sabbath to its close. Traditional travel taboos had kept the crowds away from the Saviour, but now a pathetic procession of sufferers and friends wound slowly along the lakeshore. The stillness of the evening was shattered by eager chatter and demonic shrieks.

Far into the night Jesus moved quietly among the throngs around his house. Compassionately sharing this woeful weight of suffering, He sighed and prayed, touched and smiled. Deliverance and healing flowed like a river of life. Many once weak and troubled folk returned home to spend the rest of the night telling what the Prophet of Nazareth had done for them.

At last Jesus was able to retire to His room; but only for a few hours. It was still dark when He slipped out of the house and found His way to the familiar lonely spot. Here He would refresh His spirit in prayer.

Simon and company by this time knew where to find Him; they assumed He would come back to the crowds. But they were wrong. During His prayer He had received other directions. "Let us go into the next towns, that I may preach there also: for therefore came I forth" (Mark 1:38). In communion with His Father He had learned His plans for the day. His prayer had brought Him *guidance*.

Once again it was evening. The grassy plain was thick with people. Earlier the Master had chosen this place because it was remote, isolated. His little group had secretly brought Him there by boat. But the crowds soon located Him and came hiking around the lake. Sure, it was tiring, but who cares?

Absorbed by His teaching and sunning themselves in the warm radiance of that shepherd heart, the people forgot everything—even food. Suddenly, a cold breeze hinted the approach of night. The disciples came to with a jolt. Concerned, they begged Jesus to send the folk home at once, but He had other plans. He was about to share a lad's forgotten lunch with those hungry thousands.

The miracle agreed perfectly with the people's idea of what that Prophet could do. Glowing spiritually, and full up physically, they were ready for anything. "He's the one we want for our leader," they were saying. "Let's make him king and throw out the Romans."

Jesus sensed this emotional tide. Their inborn desire for freedom was right, but He knew *this* was not the way to true liberty. Quickly He urged His disciples into the boat and back to Bethsaida. Then deliberately turning, He struck out alone for a gaunt hillside—to pray. Seen by none but His Father, the storm of temptation beat itself out (Mark 6:46). Prayer was His great resort *when tempted*.

More than once Jesus made known that His preaching and healing was a costly ministry: virtue went out of Him. Those who pour themselves out for others know the reality of this ebb tide. What was the Saviour's remedy?

When "enormous crowds collected to hear Jesus and to be healed of their diseases . . . he slipped quietly away to deserted places for prayer" (Luke 5:15, 16, Phillips). Prayer was His *supreme means of renewal.*

The people's response to the ministry of Christ was twofold. With some, His popularity increased daily; but with the religious authorities, His position grew more and more dangerous. One section misunderstood Him; the other understood Him only too well. He saw that while He was still alive He must train special men as preachers to continue His work. He would have to call them from their jobs and send them out in His own name to preach and heal. He knew that a heavy responsibility would rest upon those, so He began to prepare Himself in order to make the right selection. "It was in these days that He went off to the hillside to pray. He spent the whole night in prayer to God, and when the day broke he summoned his disciples, choosing twelve of them, to whom he gave the name of 'apostles'" (Luke 6:12, Moffatt). He *selected His co-workers* after prayer.

On another occasion, Jesus and His men were passing through the wooded hillsides of Caesarea Philippi. During a rest break, Jesus went apart to pray. Little did the others know the burden He carried. He was about to put *the* question to them, and a whole world hung on their reply. It was imperative to know if His disciples were fully convinced that He was the Messiah. He *must* know their convictions before He could show them more of His plans. The timing of this question was all-important.

He rose from His knees and confronted them: the moment had come. His intense eyes searched their faces as He spoke.

"Whom do men say that I the Son of man am?" This was just a feeler to condition their minds for the more searching probe. They told Him:

"Some say . . . John the Baptist: some, Elias; and others, Jeremias, or one of the prophets." This was the consensus; He knew that. Now, for the leading question:

"But whom say ye that I am?" Patiently—almost with an ache—He waited. What did these men, His chosen apostles, think about Him? After a long moment, Simon replied: "Thou art the Christ, the Son of the living God" (Matthew 16:16). Little did he realize the worldwide effect these ten words would have or how momentous they were for the future church of Jesus Christ.

Jesus was encouraged; He sighed with satisfaction. Having graduated, His men were now ready for the teaching of the next grade. This would be more difficult, for He had to tell them that shortly He would be leaving for Jerusalem where suffering and death awaited Him. He wanted them to know too that three days after His death He would come back to life. He knew there was a psychological moment for such disclosures as these. He *discovered these strategic times* in prayer.

Standing by the rock-hewn tomb in which lay the remains of Lazarus, Jesus lifted His eyes to heaven in prayer. "Father," He said, "I thank thee for listening to me. (I knew thou wouldst always listen to me, but I spoke on account of the crowd around that they might believe thou hast sent me.) (John 11:41, 42, Moffatt). The last few words were perhaps a whispered soliloquy. Then with a swift command He brought Lazarus back to life.

Prayer, we learn, may be neither supplication or thanksgiving but a spiritual expression and thought for those at hand. Jesus prayed *for the sake of others*.

He prayed for His disciples. For Simon Peter, He asked God to keep his faith from failing.

Christ was baptized—while praying.

On the mount, He was transfigured—as He prayed.

The agonies of the cross were anticipated by strong cryings and prayers.

Impaled upon the cross, He supplicated for the forgiveness of His tormentors. The final committal of His spirit to God was through prayer.

Lord, teach us to pray.

Our Lord's example has been set before us. We must now descend from this mount to the plains of our everyday living, bringing with us inspiration from the hills of God.

The waking hour for many men is regarded as the day's most important time. These are pregnant moments when the heart can be delicately harmonized with God, the pace set for the day, and the whole being dedicated to God for His will. No spacecraft needs more careful launching than does a minister on his daily course. Great is the need for watchfulness—right here. More than one ministerial failure knows the rot set in long before his collapse through neglect of the morning tryst.

Through the night the body and conscious mind have been resting. Normally, we awake refreshed and ready for the demands of another day. It is a thrill to know that all our faculties—graciously renewed by God in those few hours—can now be presented to Him as a living sacrifice. Every detail of life is consciously invested with divine significance if surrendered each day to your Master. No later praying seems to capture the pristine blessing of that early hour. The freeways of the mind then are clear. In a little while they will be jammed with thoughts, bumper to bumper.

This tryst, moreover, is not just for praying to God; it is for tuning in to the quiet voice of the Holy Spirit. He speaks. Fellowship is two-way communication. In the early morning, a well-kept lawn has a rare beauty. Those sturdy little blades, sparkling with dew, seem newborn each day. In a few hours the sun may scorch them and

children may jump on them; that first beauty will go. So
with the soul: that first morning hour offers unique opportunity for communion with the Lord. Bishop Ken, in his
great hymn, catches the idea:

> Awake, my soul, and with the sun
> Thy daily stage of duty run;
> Shake off dull sloth, and joyful rise
> To pay thy morning sacrifice.
>
> Direct, control, suggest, this day,
> All I design, or do, or say;
> That all my powers, with all their might,
> In Thy sole glory may unite.

A minister, especially, should realize his stewardship of
time. What right have we to break into a new day without
first acknowledging Him who gave it and spared us to
see it? Isn't it presumptuous to embark upon the day's
course with its unknown possibilities and dangers without
deliberately casting ourselves on the tender mercies of
God?

But what serenity of mind follows when the morning
tryst has been kept. Apart from the sheer satisfaction of
an audience with our King, there is a sense of preparedness
and poise that every minister needs. Emergency calls
will not overtake him unawares; neither will discouragement deflect or defeat him. The lines of communication
with heaven will be open and clear. The Spirit of the
Master will be in him and the mantle of God upon him.
He goes to answer the calls, not casually, but with com-
posure and confidence in his God. Unquestionably, the
morning tryst is uniquely important. It is during this
time of sacred intercourse that the soul really gets to
know God.

Alone with God.

Here, the real man is exposed. Wherever else there
may be camouflage, there can be none here. Oliver
Wendell Holmes said that in every man there are

various men. There is the man as he sees himself; then, as he appears to others. There is the man as he is seen by God. The closet is the place of true self-exposure. It is sorely needed by the one concerned about his public image. Life is full, not only of double-talk, but double-living: with many, the true self rarely emerges. God be thanked, in the morning watch the bared soul—the real man—can draw close to the eternal Spirit. "Search me, O God, and know my heart: try me, and know my thoughts: and see if there be any wicked way in me, and lead me in the way everlasting" (Psalm 139:23, 24).

Alone with God.

O may He lay His fashioning hand upon me. While my heart is tender and my will pliable, let Him bend or break, shape, and strengthen. Do this every day, O Lord. Let the morning watch be a surgery. I trust Thy hands; they were torn for me; they will not rend me. O to be like Thee.

Alone with God.

Then, if He sees the need, He will whisper that word of encouragement; and because it comes from Him, I shall be strengthened.

The morning tryst will bring priceless enrichment to your ministry. The way God's messages come to a man of God is quite remarkable. Sermons can sprout anytime; but when they are born during the morning watch, they seem distinctive, so undeniably God-given, as though the germinal thought were dropped in the mind—personally—by God. If these seedling thoughts are patiently gathered and committed to paper, they can be developing in the fertile soil of the mind until they are needed for further treatment. Then when comes the time for the delivery of the message, the wonder of that holy hour will somehow be shared with the congregation.

Those hearers will feel their preacher has come straight from the presence of the Lord.

Through the morning watch something else grows—slowly but unmistakeably. It is an awareness, subtle but constant, of the presence of God: an inner, sentient knowledge that His unction is upon the life and ministry. It carries the preacher through without hesitation so that when he has finished preaching, he knows something has been effected. It is more than this. When a man has experienced it, he is incomplete and unsatisfied without it.

What counsel can be offered to those desirous of making this blessed tryst an integral part of their Christian life?

There must be first a sincere purpose of heart to live for God—and this must be renewed and reaffirmed continually. It must be kept green. If this purpose is dominant, then every means for accomplishing it will be used. Perhaps this ideal has been lost or overgrown. Uncover it. Gaze at it once more until its glory begins to fascinate you again. Confess your loss to God; humble yourself before Him and do not be in a hurry. Seek Him. Ask of Him grace for a fresh and glowing start.

Then resolve to give Him first place, including that first hour of the day. "O God, Thou art my God: early will I seek Thee." Resolution is necessary, for grace will not carry you beyond your own willingness. Quietly, but definitely, make that resolve—before God. Say it aloud, but in humble dependence on Him. A decision like this helps in a crisis.

Now habit can help you. For the first few mornings the thrust of your resolution and the glow of your fresh consecration will exert their own power. You will rise with an urge. This vitality may last for a short or longer period. The real test will come later when it may seem the morning tryst is becoming a routine affair. Here is sincerity's hardest trial and here can be the place of triumph. To rise from bed—against natural inclination—and seek God without the emotion of a newly discovered pleasure, will result in a spiritual and moral victory. For this time at least, your will has governed your feelings.

The joy of commencing on the plains, so to speak, and climbing the hill of communion with God is most exhilarating. Nothing can keep God from the true seeker after Him. Clouds may hide the sun from view, but they do not put it out of existence. Day by day you are forming an invaluable habit. Character is habit consolidated. The habit of prayer is worth cultivation.

Finally, deal ruthlessly with secondary claimants for this morning hour so as to keep it free for this highest purpose. Determine to give no attention to anything but the supreme purpose in hand. Make the fence around your tryst a rigid one. Do your part. God will do the rest.

> Alone with Thee, amid the mystic shadows,
> The solemn hush of nature newly born;
> Alone with Thee, in breathless adoration,
> In the calm dew and freshness of the morn.

—H. B. Stowe.

Secret prayer is the minister's mainspring.

4
MEAT

No minister should be reduced to reading the Bible just to get texts for sermons. Before being a preacher he is a believing man who needs to come to this storehouse of God for his own personal satisfaction and delight. Day by day his mind must be exposed to the living Word of God! Brainwashed, if this word can be separated from its association with torment.

This chapter will deal mainly with the mechanics of personal Bible study. Its dynamics is a renewed heart, a clear conscience, a submissive spirit, and a conscious dependence on the Holy Spirit as Teacher. If a minister needs to major in any one thing, it is this; for "the Scriptures are the comprehensive equipment of the man of God, and fit him fully for all branches of his work" (2 Timothy 3:17, Phillips). An anomaly is a preacher of the Word who fails to steep his mind and heart in the Word.

A minister must be convinced that all Scripture is "inspired of God." Mercy help him if he flounders here, for he will be holding a blunt sword with a loose handle in his paralyzed hand. It would be better if he decided to offer his help to human beings through some other vocation. He must as a preacher have confidence in his authority.

But if he is assured of the Bible's divine inspiration, he will have all he needs for "teaching the Faith and correcting error, [and] for resetting the direction of a man's life and training him in good living" (2 Timothy 3:16, Phillips).

READ THE BIBLE

Read it *silently*, lovingly, as a devotional incentive, with the ears of your heart open to what God, the Lord, will speak. Choose undisturbed moments for this if you want to catch that gentle inner voice. It is important to feel that God is speaking to you—personally. Pore over His words as if you were reading a love letter.

> Speak, Lord, in Thy stillness,
> While I wait on Thee;
> Hushed my heart to listen
> In expectancy.
> —E. M. Grimes.

Read it *aloud*. This helps to overcome the bane of familiarity with the sacred Book. Much of significant value slips past us because of this. The slower, more precise, audible reading will often be like a fresh voice in a group discussion: it will bring a new shade of thought. It is well to capture these ideas in a notebook kept close at hand for that purpose.

In addition, this provides excellent practice in enunciation and expression—arts sadly lacking in some pulpits. A minister can feel gratified when a worshiper thanks him for the clear and meaningful way in which he read the Bible during the service.

For young people, reading audibly will help them over

the scare of hearing their own voices. One day they may be given the honor of reading the Scriptures in public; then such practice as this provides will certainly reduce tension; it may even save them fluffing.

Read it in *fragments*. Chapters are divisions of convenience, but they are not divinely inspired. So, when finishing a chapter, glance into the next to see if it belongs to its predecessor.

Read it *at length*. As a change, it is good to read two or three short books, or one long prophecy, at a sitting. The panoramic as well as the local view is necessary. Often when studying shorter passages for pulpit treatment, you will find the Holy Spirit makes use of your broader acquaintance with the Scriptures.

Read it as *God's holy Word*—authentic, authoritative, awesome. We are not asked to improve it by addition, deletion, or alteration, but to receive it with meekness.

During a time of religious persecution in Scotland, a young boy was stealthily finding his way to a secret meeting of believers. Suddenly from behind a tree stepped out an armed soldier to challenge the youth.

"And where are you going this Sunday morning, my son?" His lips curled in a sneer. The boy froze—speechless. Then like a flash it came to him.

"Sir, I'm going to hear the reading of my Father's will."

With a disbelieving stare the soldier grunted, "Pass on."

The boy was right: the Bible is a revelation of our Father's will. Within is explained the greatest and most ambitious plan of all time—the salvaging of a lost humanity.

Read it as *the world's finest literature*. The Bible has standardized the English language for all the English-speaking peoples. It is reported that in Britain before 1611, the year of the King James Version, people in different counties of England (for example, Devonshire and Yorkshire) could hardly understand one another. A wit, no doubt, might retort that this is so even yet; but he would be exaggerating.

Writing of the English Bible, Professor J. Livingston Lowes said: "It has a pithiness and raciness, a homey tang, a terse sententiousness, an idiomatic flavor which comes home to men's business and bosoms." It will increase our appreciation of this great Library if we realize it is of the highest literary significance. Its range includes history, stories, letters, sermons, parables, collections of laws, state documents, and genealogies. The stately and beautiful language of the King James Version unquestionably influenced English literature: it became a model for many authors.

Tribute to the Bible does not come only from those who love its Author. Sir William Watson, who was a skeptic in religious beliefs but a master of literature, testifies:

> Every kind of literary magnificence is supremely exemplified in the Bible. For sustained splendor and coloring the greater part of Ezekiel 27 and 28 is, probably, unapproachable. The most perfect elegy in all literature is, perhaps, David's lament for Saul and Jonathan, and at the other end of the great gamut of emotion the song of Deborah and Barak with its savage repetitions and antiphonal effects is the most superb expression of the intoxication of triumph I know. The book of Job blazes through with splendid things. It is so packed with riches that selection becomes embarrassing; chapter 38, however, reaches the summit of sublimity.

Writers, orators, even advertising men find help for their arts in this great Book. Its literature and principles are woven into the fabric of our national existence.

RECEIVE THE BIBLE

Receive it as *instruction*. Psalm 119, as most (some?) people know, is the longest in the Psalter. It is more. C. H. Spurgeon termed it "the holy soul's soliloquy before an open Bible," and added: "Our best improvement of this sacred composition will come through getting our minds into intense sympathy with its subject. In order to do this, we might do well to commit it to memory" (*Treasury of David*).

This Psalm uses at least eight figures to describe the Word of God. They are not synonomous. Here they are:

1. *The Law of the Lord,* showing the structure of God's government. Our Sovereign shows us the law of His kingdom.

2. *Commandments,* expressing God's personal desires. These are the duty, or the delight, of those who read them, depending on whether or not they are members of His kingdom.

3. *Statutes,* affirming the fixed, determined, and unchangeable principles of the Eternal. These, in sum, constitute God's law.

4. *Precepts,* teaching the duties derived from those principles.

5. *Judgments,* providing us with guiding lines in optional matters.

6. *Ways,* referring to the ordinary pathway of man, his road map.

7. *Word,* God's communication with man.

8. *Testimonies,* bearing witness to God's character and acts.

All this instruction is to be received *reverently.* This will be the normal attitude of our mind if we sincerely believe the Bible to be God's Word. The Psalm just quoted uses terms denoting reverence, deference, and submission, and shows what response God expects of us. We are responsible for keeping (not swerving from), cleaving to and longing after (not wandering from), respecting (not forgetting), observing, and standing in awe of God's Word. The wisdom instilled by the Bible is perfect; the demand it makes is total.

Yet we should receive it *happily* because it is for our good. Rejoice in it, delight in it, hope in it, and trust in it are God's counsels.

It instructs us concerning *character*. First, it works inwardly, gently molding our thinking, correcting our disposition, and upgrading our motives. What we think and believe is what we are becoming. Both in its process and in the ultimate, this transformation is miraculous. "Let God remold your minds from within" (Romans 12:2, Phillips) describes His activity when we conscientiously "read, mark, learn, and inwardly digest" Bible truth. This is the primary purpose of Bible study.

It teaches us about our *conduct*. The way we live is determined by what we believe: belief works itself out in behavior. This conduct affects our various relationships, as follows:

We are sons of God by divine authority; yet we are learning to live as sons of God by education and training. This comes to us through the Bible.

We are also members of the Body of Christ and a local church. So, our privileges and responsibilities are outlined for us in the Bible—as worshipers, warriors, and workers.

As part of a family—husband, wife, father, mother, son, or daughter—we learn our duty from the Bible.

As members of the world's brotherhood (by natural birth), our place and function are explained to us, as is our Christian attitude toward the powers that be.

The Bible points up our *privileges*. It shows us reasons for our secure standing before God, in Christ. It encourages us to draw upon the power and grace available and so live victoriously. It repeatedly reminds us of our spiritual obligations in intercession, witnessing, and giving.

Receive it as *food*. Christ, the Bread of Life, alone

can satisfy the soul's hunger. To an audience of two discouraged men, Jesus "beginning at Moses and all the prophets . . . expounded unto them in all the scriptures the things concerning himself" (Luke 24:27). Thus, we may find Christ, the True Bread, in all the Scriptures.

In the Gospels, His portrait is painted by the evangelists. As we prayerfully ponder their words, the Holy Spirit infuses life and Christ steps out of the picture—a living Personality—whose words are spirit and life. The reading experience then becomes an interview, a heart-to-heart talk with the Lord. In the Gospels, then, we see Christ *pictorially;* in the Epistles, Christ *doctrinally;* and in the Old Testament, Christ *typically.* It is Christ in all the Scriptures.

Our Lord specifically stated that the manna was a foreshadowing of Himself as divine sustenance, the heavenly Bread. This miraculous Old Testament provision has several lessons for us.

"I will rain bread from heaven for you," said Jehovah to Moses (Exodus 16:4). The Bible, like the manna, is God's gift to man. Thoughout their slow journey to Canaan, Israel was never without this heaven-sent food. Had it failed to arrive, they would have perished in the wilderness. In our western world, a copy of the Bible is available to everyone. There are countries, however, where supplies are so limited or prohibited that a single page from the beloved Book is a cherished delight. It is memorized, copied, and passed on to others who are just as eager to receive it. The continued existence and circulation of the Scriptures is certainly a gift of God.

But though God caused the manna to fall for His people, He left *them* certain things to do. *"The people shall go out and gather. . . ."* Each morning, except the Sabbath, people had to get out early because their food would melt under the sun's warmth. Could God be wanting to teach *us*—by this—that the best time for gathering spiritual food is the morning hour before the day's demands take over?

It pleased God to scatter manna round about Israel's camp. No doubt He could have had it fall in heaps by each tent and even in convenient plate-size portions. But it was a "small round thing" and had to be carefully picked up. It must have been an interesting sight each morning to see the people—backs bent—as they went about gathering their supplies. It perfectly illustrates another point: the "eat and run" approach to the Bible is out; we must be prepared to give time to it. There is so little for the hurried reader. The bent back—diligent searching and careful gathering—is what God has planned for us.

"*A certain rate every day,*" was God's further condition, dramatizing an obvious truth. Just as our bodies need regular daily meals, so do our souls. A simple but practical idea is to try and draw one original thought from the day's portion. To condense the thought to eight or ten words is an aid to exactness and concentration. You may not produce inspirational gems at first, but practice in this simple exercise will keep you alert. At least you will have something to show as the fruit of your own reading and thinking.

INVESTIGATE THE BIBLE

Some Bible readers and their habits remind us of butterflies and bees. Some readers flit from flower to flower. Others stop, penetrate, and come out loaded. Choose which you will be. The Bible stretches before you like a promised land. Go in and occupy it: possess your possessions. Here are ways to help you do so.

Make outlines of the Bible books. It is true there are books on the market in which this has been done. Why should a man go to all this bother when he can easily make use of another's labor? The answer is simple: what you quarry, you prize; it is yours. If a man is satisfied with spiritual dried eggs, that is his business; but he should not imagine he has the best. "Concentrate on winning God's approval, on being a workman with nothing to be ashamed of, and who knows how to use the word of truth to the best advantage" (2 Timothy 2:15, Phillips). Concentrate.

Pursue a theme through the Bible. A man, for instance, who in his early years gets a firm grasp of the symbolism of the Tabernacle and its meaning for Christians will have a scriptural groundwork for his entire ministry. To study such a subject for a period of months is like putting money in the bank: you can live on the interest.

The *biographical* approach will lead to a harvest field. Think of the coverage given, for example, to Abraham, Jacob, Moses, David, Peter, and Paul. It is evident God means us to learn much from such men. Again, why not embark on your own personal study of the Man?

There are *keys words* such as redemption, believed, life, etc. Why not brood over this gold? Key words will unlock Holy Writ.

The titles or *names of God* beckon you—indeed, should lure you. Ultimately a Christian's worship is according to his high or low thoughts of God. A serious study like this could never be completed, but it would purify and elevate your concept of God.

In all study we meet up with problems and questions. Some cannot be resolved immediately. These can be temporarily laid aside to await the further light that comes in due time, as God sees we are ready to receive it. A great advantage of regular, systematic reading of the Word is that it explains itself if the student is patient.

MEDITATE ON THE BIBLE

Messages written in invisible ink often require warmth to make them visible. It takes the warmth of personal need to bring out the hidden meaning of "this book of the law."

"Thou shalt meditate therein day and night," was the Lord's command to Joshua, Israel's new leader. A further advantage of utilizing the morning hour for Bible study is that we have food for thought for the remainder of the day. Whether traveling, doing routine jobs, eating, or just before dropping off to sleep, we have a thought stabilizer working for us.

"That thou mayest observe to do according to all that is written therein: for then thou shalt make thy way prosperous, and then thou shalt have good success" (Joshua 1:8). No more inspiring promise was ever given to an aspiring leader. The man of the Word will become the man of God, truly prosperous and eminently successful.

Means

A rightly conducted examination of God's Word will be found to yield not only rich results in homiletics and hermeneutics, but in apologetics. In the structure and contents of Holy Scripture may be found a triumphant answer to all assaults upon its inspiration and authority as a divine Book and the standard of doctrine and duty. The Bible is its own witness; and, whoever, turning from all external defences to the Book itself, will seek to make himself master of its contents and to enter sympathetically into its spirit, will find himself lodged in an impregnable fortress where he laughs in derision at all who, like Voltaire, threaten to overthrow it, while he holds in scarcely less contempt the timidity which fears such threats. The Ark of the Covenant needs no help from puny human hands to steady it, nor is the Shekinah fire in danger of being quenched by those who blow upon it to put it out. Light needs only to be let shine and it becomes its own witness. A lion has only to be let loose and he needs no defender. Give the Word of God free course and it will be victor over all assault.

—Arthur T. Pierson
Knowing the Scriptures

5

MEANS

Sermon: "a lecture or serious talk on behaviour, responsibility, etc., especially a long, tedious, annoying one." Webster offers this as one meaning of the word. In doing so he reflects a typical attitude, one that goes along with "don't preach at me." But it is not unusual for the good to be castigated; the average person, of course, hardly likes to think about anything of a serious nature if he can help it.

On the other hand, it has been said that a sermon is not an argument to be followed, but an event to be experienced. That event is an encounter with the living God.

So, here we have the two extreme views.

In *The Burden of the Lord,* Ian Macpherson points out that the Greek word *logos* (in John's Gospel) is translated in the Latin version of the New Testament as *sermo,* a term from which sermon is derived. "To feel the full force of this striking fact," says the writer, "it is necessary to study the prologue to the Fourth Gospel . . . putting the word *sermo* in the place of Word, wherever it occurs. Listen: In the beginning was the Sermon and the Sermon was with God and the Sermon was God."

Think of this: it might be said that Jesus Christ was God's sermon.

However that may be, a sermon is a tool, the preacher a craftsman. He is to become adept in sharpening and using his instrument. This obviously entails both a continuing education and constant practice.

In the Bible, God has given us the fullest range of truth that humans can comprehend. It is the work of the minister to get to understand and apply that truth to his hearers. This is best done "line upon line and precept upon precept." As a minister "addicts" himself to this work and waits upon God for his ministry, he will be blessed with guidance and help in his preparation. His messages will touch prevailing needs and fit local conditions. Making this application of truth requires skill and understanding. He can rejoice that God will give His wisdom to those that ask for it.

If he is unconcerned or careless in his preparatory study, the preacher can expect a casual hearing. If his sermons, however, are honestly thought out and attractively presented, they will be well received and their message, in part at least, retained.

Homiletics has to do with the preparation and preaching of a sermon, especially the layout or disposition of its parts, its structure.

The skills of homiletics, through diligent practice and with God's help, will bring you the ability to interpret, illustrate, and apply the truth. There are many who can see truth for themselves but are not able to explain it in a simple way to others. There is a difference.

A novice was invited to preach in the church of a seasoned minister. After the service, the young man waited for the pulpit giant to pass judgment on his sermon. When after some while the matter was not even mentioned, he took his courage in both hands and broached the subject. "Well," mused the older man in a kind voice, "let me put it like this. For thirty minutes you were trying to get something out of *your* head—instead of putting something into *mine.*" It is doubtful if that lesson was ever forgotten.

Training in homiletics will discipline the mind to think . . . search . . . grapple . . . coordinate . . . illustrate, and aim with purpose. Advocating diligent practice in this craft has been called "the gospel of the treadmill." Do not disdain it because it seems far removed from the memorable moment of your divine call or the sacred scenes of your ordination. These mountaintop experiences were to stimulate you for the more arduous work in the valley; less exciting, maybe, but highly productive.

Jeremiah's experience illustrates this. God launched him with a unique commission and a fiery enduement: his own testimony shows this. Boldly he claims, "the Lord put forth his hand, and touched my mouth. And the Lord said unto me, Behold, I have put my words in thy mouth. See, I have this day set thee over the nations and over the kingdoms, to root out, and to pull down, and to destroy, and to throw down, to build and to plant" (Jeremiah 1:9, 10). With the echo of these dynamic, frightening words in his soul, he waited tensely for the next step.

It came as an anticlimax—just a small branch from an almond tree crossing his line of vision. Could an ordinary twig be in any way related to those previous phenomena? But God asked, "What seest thou?" The divine afflatus quickens the vision and sharpens the insights.

This is a penetrating question for all preachers:

WHAT SEEST THOU?

What seest thou? Here is the need for *clarity.* God's

truth must throb with meaning for us—first. *What do* we see in our studying? What is the central truth—the heart of this message I am preparing? What is God saying here? Has it got through to me yet? Let me look again and again.

What *seest* thou? Here is the need for *concentration.* The almond tree was familiar enough; a closer, longer look was required before it would yield its message from God. We have to pore over and ponder deeply the familiar wording of the Bible before it will yield its inner meaning. And for Jeremiah, what a message it was! God is ever watching over his Word to perform it.

The ministry of the Word calls for concentration. Study demands strength and time; it should have our best. "In my judgment," said Clarence E. Macartney, "the reason many preachers fail to make an impression, secure results and fulfill their own high ambitions is their lack of ability to concentrate. Deep concentration means that one must be willing to be much alone."

What seest *thou?* Here is the need for *convictions.* A preacher must have more in his message than "I don't believe this," or "I'm against that." He also needs more than a denominational persuasion. He must struggle through to convictions of his own. These are built slowly, often painfully through the years, like the aggregations of a coral reef. "Believe me," wrote the disenchanted G. Campbell Morgan, "the most difficult task is to get people to believe the things they think they do believe." He was right.

Clarity, concentration, and convictions: Jeremiah passed his examination. The question is. . . ?

This author's first attempt at serious writing for publication—surprisingly—was successful. The magazine editor even asked for more. The idea that triggered that first article was a familiar cherished family experience.

It was the second year of our marriage: we were sampling the various phases of parenthood, including a new slant on "He giveth me songs in the night." Our baby had discovered this was a good time to try our her lungs. We had certain brilliant ideas as a consequence, but none of them proved suitable for writing.

That came one day when our baby was contentedly enjoying her lunch at her mother's breast. Earlier had been those demanding cries, rising in crescendo, as the feeding hour approached. Then came the contented sucking, obvious relish and complete abandon to the thrilling experience.

Words clutched at the mind . . . "As newborn babes, desire the sincere milk of the word. . . ." We saw it in our infant, an inborn, voracious appetite demanding satisfaction and suitable food readily available: both created by God.

Her mother's milk was rich in every needed ingredient: adult diet was simplified by the mother's digestion and available as milk. It was *food that had passed through the digestion of another.*

This rather beautifully describes a sermon too. "Give ye them to eat," Jesus challenged His men. "Send them away, that they may . . . buy themselves bread," was the best human solution to the hunger problem of the five thousand.

"See that your 'flock of God' is *properly* fed," urges an undershepherd at the command of the Chief Shepherd (1 Peter 5:2, Phillips). Talking of sheep—"feed 'em little, feed 'em often, and feed 'em warm," is a shepherd's advice. It has a message for pastors too.

A sermon, then, can be thought of as food that has passed through the digestion of another—your mental digestion or meditative processes. What you and your text have lived and thought through will put strong ingredients in your sermon. As a preacher, you should train your sermonic digestion to work at all times. Walking and talking with your text or passage will help to break it down into smaller and simpler parts. The tendrils of your mind will have time to feel for and fasten on illustrative experiences deep within yourself. You will be eating the Word and savoring its taste by mastication. Your digestive juices will be giving it enzyme treatment: you will continue your study simmering with ideas.

We have used a simple analogy to define a sermon. Here is Phillips Brooks' way of putting it:

> Preaching is the communication of truth by men to men. Truth through personality is our description of real preaching. The truth must come really through the person, not merely over his lips, not merely into his understanding and out through his pen. It must come through His character, his affections, his whole intellectual and moral being. It must come genuinely through him.

This means that a true sermon is not usually the work of an hour. It is not the hasty scrambling together of random thoughts or related texts after the wearing activities of the week are over. Such a snack will be heavy, unappetizing, and indigestible. On your desk might stand a motto reminding you to "concentrate . . . on your reading and on your preaching and teaching. Give your whole attention, all your energies, to these things, so that your progress is plain for all to see. Keep a critical eye both upon your own life and on the teaching you give, and if you continue to follow the line I have indicated you will not only save your own soul but the souls of many of your hearers as well" (1 Timothy 4:13, 15, 16, Phillips).

Food through another's digestion, truth through personality—here are two related views of the sermon. And they are near the thought of the Eternal too.

"In the beginning was the Word, and the Word was with God, and the Word was God" (John 1:1). These majestic, mountainous words declare the eternity, relationship, and deity of the Son of God—the living Word. In a restricted sense—though with equal force—they describe the written Word, the Bible; for Christ is enfolded in the Bible.

John continues, "And the Word was made flesh, and dwelt among us" (John 1:14). History's most amazing fact, the incarnation of the Son of God, is described in nine words, words which also tell how the written Word is to be transmitted to our people. The Word—by becoming incarnate in the preacher—comes through him, clothed with his flesh and then is mediated in preaching to the hearers.

Yet, gloriously it is not only the written Word that is so transmitted, but the living Word who by the Spirit is revealed in and communicated through the written Word and the preacher. Preaching Christ is mediating Christ.

This elevates preaching to the level of a sublime and supernatural act. It makes it—to use Bernard Manning's phrase—"a manifestation of the Incarnate Word, from the Written Word, by the spoken word."

Well may angels covet to be preachers of the Word.

Materials

No man can be a consistently effective preacher who begrudges the time which pulpit preparation takes. The wisest use of his time is one of the major problems with any minister of God.

To begin with, he is largely a master of his own time. That is both a privilege and a peril. No one—unless it be the Recording Angel—takes heed of his hour of beginning work, nor with what resolution he goes at it till the day is done. It is not the least of the responsibilities placed upon him by ordination that, in the main, he may order his own life.

—E. W. Sangster
The Approach to Preaching

6
MATERIALS

We turn our attention now to the long-range preparation for our pulpit work. This is sometimes called permanent preparation. A sermon is the product of years. E. M. Bounds said it takes twenty years to make a preacher; this is why many sermons have a long pregnancy.

If preaching is "truth through personality," then each message as you preach it will have a unique aura. In composing a sermon you draw upon all that is within you—all you have experienced, received, and are.

Nature's womb is the soil. Replete with chemical deposits of many years and alive with bacteria, it waits to germinate the sown seed and nurture the tiny plant. The preacher's mind, stored with the learning and experiences of previous years and constantly activated by his reading, is the germinal soil of his sermons. This is where his seedlings grow. Here he must be always cultivating.

Systematic study of the Bible, therefore, is imperative. A minister needs to lock himself in his study with his Bible. First, because his own spiritual development and culture depend on it. Then, because this Word of the living God is the source of his message and declaring it with a "thus saith the Lord" is his solemn duty.

This constant digging into the Scripture must not be left to mood or inclination. It must be pursued relentlessly and endlessly, though at times it may seem like drudgery. A man is not worth his salt as a minister unless he knows toil, sweat, and conflict while girding himself to preach. "God will surely curse that minister who lumbers up and down the world all the week, and then thinks to prepare for his pulpit by a hurried hour or two on Saturday night. God knows Saturday night were little enough time in which to weep and pray and to get his sinful soul into a fit frame of mind for the approaching day." These searching but not too severe words of Thomas Shepherd, Pilgrim Father and founder of Harvard University, should haunt every minister, beginner or teacher.

James Black, in the *Mystery of Preaching*, calls this hard digging work the "gospel of the treadmill." "It means," he says, "being in your study, with your jacket off ... sheer grim work among your books." "A man's future," he declares, "does not come to him out of tomorrow, but out of yesterday." It may be necessary in these times when many enjoy the luxury of air conditioning to point out that "jacket off" used to be synonymous to hard work: stripped for action. Every preacher hopes for that special momentary inspiration that at times overtakes him when he is preaching. But it is foolish to imagine this is meant to replace his diligent hammering at the Word when he is alone—and unseen—in his study. "Cases are won in chambers," is a dictum of the legal profession. There is no excuse for unpreparedness in the courtroom. It is equally true of the pulpit.

A minister is more likely to enjoy the afflatus of the Spirit while preaching if he has been painstaking in study. It is pathetically uncomfortable watching an ill-prepared pulpiteer struggling to raise the wind and get airborne by flapping his wings. Tongue-in-the-cheek advice for such is: "If you don't strike oil in ten minutes stop boring."

What we are here urging is that study must become a habit; it is already a responsibility. Self-discipline and concentration are imperative. Writing of this need, Floyd Doud Shafer says:

> Rip out his telephone, burn up his ecclesiastical success sheets, refuse his glad hand, and put water in the gas tank of his community buggy. Give him a Bible and tie him in his pulpit and make him preach the Word of the living God. Test him, quiz him and examine him; humiliate him for his ignorance of things divine, and shame him for his glib comprehension of finances, batting averages, and political in-fighting. Laugh at his frustrated effort to play psychiatrist, scorn his insipid morality, refuse his supine intelligence, ignore his broadmindedness which is only flathead-edness, and compel him to be a minister of the Word. . . . Form a choir and raise a chant and haunt him with it night and day: 'Sir, we wish to see Jesus.' When, at long last, he dares assay the pulpit, ask him if he has a word from God; if he does not, then dismiss him and tell him you can read the morning paper, digest the television commentaries, think through the day's superficial problems, manage the community's myriad drives, and bless assorted baked potatoes and green beans ad infinitum better then he can. . . . Let him be totally ignorant of the down-street gossip, but give him a chapter and order him to walk around it, camp on it, suffer with it, and come at last to speak it backwards and forwards until all he says about it rings with the truth of eternity.*

In this chapter we will suggest ways to go after, capture, and store as resource material, experiences and events that rush by us in the pageant of life.

Read, read, read. Don't build a library, read books. The

*Floyd Doud Shafer, "And Preach as You Go," *Christianity Today,* March 27, 1961, p. 8.

well-filled shelves of a minister friend have at times made us envious. The perfect arrangement of the volumes and the warm dignity of their spines imparts an aura of study to a room. Yet those books somehow look too tidy—as if they were rarely thumbed. A comment in appreciation of the fine collection draws the confession: "I'm afraid I haven't read most of them."

The early years of one's ministry should be gratefully used for purposeful reading. Responsibilities are lighter in the smaller church and outside engagements fewer. So now is the time to live with the masters.

Read, not to steal another's sermons, but to provoke your own thinking and avoid becoming self-opinionated and blinkered. As a dividend, you will find many choice illustrations for coming days.

If you are reading a borrowed book, you will need to write out the quotations and illustrations you wish to keep. To read a book of spiritual or intellectual worth without making notes is to let gold slip through your fingers. A minister, regretting this defect of his earlier years, laments, "I was too lazy to roast what I took in hunting." Be a notemaker.

If the book is yours, here is a way to conserve its valuable material. As you commence reading, let a sheet of paper journey with you through the volume. Now, make a short note of the illustrative material you wish to retain as you come to it—subject by subject. At the end you will have a page of notes, your own digest for future use. It might look something like this:

> Creation: the interval, 15, 18, 53
> Scriptures: inspiration of, 14
> Lucifer: 21
> Will: only one in eternity, 29, 37
> Sin: origin of, 31
> Bishop: origin of word, 31
> God: names of, 50

Man: depravity of, 115, 125
Election: illustrated, 120
Death: what is a dead soul? 125

What to do next with these notes will be described later in the chapter.

You will want to keep *clippings* from papers and magazines, etc.; but unless you have an uncanny memory, you will soon forget what is on your disorderly pile. They must be classified, indexed in some way, and filed. These details will be explained later.

Now we come to scores of incidents we *observe* in the panorama of our passing days. The pitch and toss of life stirs up happenings all around us, more than we can possibly remember. As preachers, we must train ourselves to assess those happenings that will help us bring God's Word, more understandably, to the people. Always carry a small loose-leaf notebook with you so that you can capture these intriguing but elusive incidents on the spot. Here is counsel directed to writers, but it is equally suitable for preachers:

1. Record—without waiting for impressions.
Be specific; let the notes be detailed.
2. Take a good look at a few things.
3. Analyze unusual experiences afterwards.
4. Search for possible meanings.

This means full notes are to be made as soon after the event as possible. Be discriminating: time will not allow you to record all you see.

What follows is most important: the analysis and interpretation of what you have seen. Asking yourself questions frees the imagination. You watch the world's stage through the eyes of a Christian—and more—a Christian preacher. What is the meaning of this? you ask. Why did it happen this way? What Biblical truth does it bring to mind? Is there a text that is relevant? Could I use this for illustrating a sermon? What does it illustrate?

The notes should be given a classifying title so they can be filed. The method of recalling them will be discussed later.

There are *parables* seen in everyday life. During a Bible-teaching campaign we were staying in a motel close to a supermarket. From one window we could see shoppers pushing their loaded buggies through the electronic doors and heading for their cars. They had chosen and paid for what they needed and were now taking it home for family use.

Another window overlooked the rear of the market. This scene was entirely different. From early morning onward huge produce trucks were rolling up and unloading supplies in bulk. We saw how vital it was these ingoing supplies should continue. The average shopper probably never gave a thought to the supply until some emergency held up deliveries.

How important, too, that when Christians come to church—a filling station—they should get plenty of the needed basic food. (It was food, chiefly, that customers came for, not giveaways or gimmicks.) How necessary, therefore, that a pastor should have constant incoming supplies of God's food so that he can give it out generously.

Contacts with men, women, and children furnish dynamic illustrations to the preacher if he is on the lookout for them. London has a fine subway system called the Underground or, colloquially, the Tube. One day we watched a little girl on an underground platform, obviously for the first time. Her eyes were dancing with excitement. She gripped her father with both hands—happily scared. A train rumbled in the distance. The child clung more tightly, her eyes glued to the dark circle where the mysterious tunnel yielded to the brilliant lights of the platform. The rumble grew louder. Suddenly, out from the black hole the squat train roared into the station.

Spellbound, the child didn't know what to expect next. Then her eyes became like organ stops as the compartment doors opened automatically—magically, of course—and closed again with no human touch. We couldn't help wondering if we might not have the same feelings when, as children of the Father, we are introduced—for the first time—to the sights and sounds of heaven.

Nature is lavish with her lessons. Did you ever watch a squirrel burying nuts? We were intrigued by the feverish activity of one of these furry friends as he dug out a deep nut closet. It was not an unfamiliar sight, but this time there was something different. Perhaps in the cycle of the seasons the squirrel was at a point where the instinct to bury and the urge to dig up and eat were changing over. For after he had tamped the earth into his hole, he began to scratch it out again. Uncertainly he backed off and went elsewhere—only to return, pull out the nut and scramble up a tree. You could see the decision was killing him. Maybe he needed a psychiatrist. People, even Christians, get confused when they cannot make up their minds which direction to take or which master to serve. "How long halt ye between two opinions?" Indecision is misery.

Analogies from science, lessons from the business world—even automobiles—are waiting to be caught by the keen preacher and adapted for use. He only has to be alert and willing to use notebook and pencil.

In our regular reading of the Bible we shall often linger at texts and passages that positively demand to be used in our preaching. Are we going to ignore these because they are so numerous? By no means. If we capture them now and store them, we shall be more than thankful later on. So, as a text strikes you, write it out in full at the top of a sheet of paper. Quote the reference. Underneath— then and there—add any preliminary thoughts you already have, no matter how random. If you have an idea for a simple outline, write that down too. All this is the work of a few minutes; it may save many hours.

These sheets of textual notes should be kept together in a big file. You can call this your stockpot, if you like, in honor of the big stewpan grandmother used to have standing on the wood stove. All the tidbits of this and that were dropped into her stockpot and gently simmered. You might wonder what the stew would taste like, but it always had that yummy flavor.

Locked in your study at some future time when you are inspirationally becalmed and perspiration is the order of the day, you will give thanks for your friendly stockpot. Thoughtfully leafing through those sheets of notes you will discover the germ of a worthwhile sermon. Maybe you will have the delight similar to that of a squirrel when he finds a nut in winter.

By now it is evident we must have a method of recording all this valuable material: a central room.

Earlier in the chapter we suggested that when reading one of your own books you should make a list of topical material you wish to record (see page 67). This list can now be transferred to a card index.

First, you number your book. You can list your books and their numbers at the beginning of your card index. This will in time be the key to your library.

Now you take your paper with list of topics. The first item to record is "Creation: the interval, 15, 18, 53." Turning to your card index, you look up CREATION. If you do not already have a card for this subject, prepare one. Write CREATION at the top and make your entry on the first line: "the interval, 1/15, 18, 53." When you refer to this in the future, the first number will give you the title of the book and subsequent numbers the pages in that book.

All this is not as complicated as it sounds. The benefits, of course, are reaped after a few years of patiently storing away the cream of your reading. One day, instead of scratching your head and saying, "Where did I read that?" or, possibly, standing by your shelves and flipping page after page trying to track down elusive information, you will get at it in seconds and be rewarded for your diligence.

Now let us think about your clippings. You have already classified them and they are ready to be put into appropriate folders for your filing cabinet. Before this takes place, however, they should be noted in your card index. For example, suppose you have clipped an article about EVOLUTION. Before dropping it into a folder so designated, refer to EVOLUTION in your cards. Perhaps you already have one in use; if so, you simply record the article and author and add the word FILE. Years later you will be delighted to rediscover the article by means of your index.

The notes in your small loose-leaf notebook can be recorded and filed in the same way. You may not require them for many days or, possibly, never, but by diligently working at it you are accumulating precious resources and making them readily available.

"Wide reading, perceptive observation, reflective thinking, interacting conversations, disciplined Bible study and communion with the Holy Spirit," these are fruitful fields for your permanent preparation.

Mirror

I heard one say the other day that a certain preacher had no more gifts for the ministry than an oyster, and in my judgment this was a slander on the oyster, for that worthy bivalve shows great descretion in his openings, and knows when to close. If some men were sentenced to hear their own sermons it would be a righteous judgment upon them, and they would soon cry out with Cain, "My punishment is greater than I can bear." Let us not fall under the same condemnation.

—C. H. Spurgeon
Lectures to My Students

7

MIRROR

Dust settles on the covers of hundreds of Bibles. Many people—even some Christians, unfortunately—leave the Bible alone; they say it is too difficult to understand. We must not dismiss this as nonsensical.

To start with, not everyone enjoys reading—even a child's book. There are, indeed, parts of the Bible that are not simple, either in language or teaching. Yet how can its divine principles be learned without its contents being read? A Christian cannot live vigorously without the Bread of Life, or purposefully without the Guidebook. As preachers, therefore, our duty is clear. We have to find simple ways of expressing the unchanging truth to our generation and making the Bible as fascinating as, say, the *Reader's Digest*.

It is a fundamental of education that people more readily accept that which is closely related to themselves. The preacher has to put them in the picture. When a barber has finished trimming our hair, he flourishes a mirror behind our head. This, with the help of the glass in front of us, gives us an all-round view. In our preaching we set the Biblical looking glass in front of the people: it is imperative we do so. Then, by using a second reflector —the mirror of apt illustration—we help people see themselves in the picture.

However, a warning is necessary right here. There is a kind of preaching that is nothing more than a recital of well-worn anecdotes tied together loosely with Scripture verses. The congregation that has to endure the repetitious elaboration of such stories is to be pitied. Let it be emphatically stated that illustrations only merit mention in a sermon when their telling rolls up a blind and lets light stream into the mind. They are no compensation for lack of study or a wobbly sermon structure.

Having said that, we now turn to consider their legitimate use and undeniable value.

An illustration can help to *establish rapport* with an audience. This may not be necessary if a preacher is with his own flock, but if he is in new territory it may ease his hearers into mental unison with him. This is most desirable.

Illustrations help to *make abstract truth clear and vivid.* Bible doctrine doesn't have to be lumpy: it can quietly fall and soak like the dew. It depends on the way it is presented. Clarity is the all-important secret of success in preaching-teaching. Clear thinking and speaking cuts through mental fog like nothing else. Time spent on making things plain is well used. That is why writing for speakers is as beneficial as exercise for the overweight. It cuts down verbiage and makes every word merit its place. This, of course, reduces the confusion. Words perfectly clear to the speaker may not always be understood by the hearer:

A doctor advised a foreign patient to drink hot water an hour before breakfast every morning. After a week, he asked him if he felt better.

"I feel worse, if anything," the patient complained.

"Well, did you follow my directions," asked the doctor, "and drink hot water an hour before breakfast every morning?" "I tried my best, doctor, but I couldn't keep it up for more than fifteen minutes at a time."

Illustrations heighten color and *add interest.* You can feel a zoom as minds get the boost of this new stimulus. Those important people in your congregation—the children—catch up with you when you tell a story.

Illustrations *make sermons stick.* Knowledge of doctrine is not an end in itself. Doctrine and duty must walk hand in hand. An adroit illustration will put feet on an article of belief.

When a certain lawyer raised a point of doctrine, "Who is my neighbor?" the Master used a superb illustration—the immortal story of the Good Samaritan. This, of course, was so well told that the lawyer answered his own question. But Jesus did not let him go without showing him his duty: "Go thou and do likewise." The lawyer had looked into the mirror and seen himself.

Illustrations provide a *mental break* for the audience. As the sermon moves from point to point, listeners are climbing the hill called "concentration." Mental muscles are getting a workout and may be getting tired. The preacher realizes this but also knows that in a moment he will rivet his point with an illustration. The change of style is like stopping for a "breather." Muscles relax, faces crease into smile, heads nod agreement. The light of wonderment shines in the eyes of a young Christian and the preacher thanks God and takes courage. With strength gained through momentary relaxation the audience prepares to finish the climb.

Illustrations are *persuasive.* The appeal of many a fine exposition has been sharpened by a well-told incident. Maybe this final featherweight has turned the balance after explanation, argument, and appeal have made their thrust.

Here, then, are some of the advantages of using illustrations in preaching. To have such a tool, the preacher will be willing to work hard and long.

The butterfly collector with his cabinets of beautiful specimens has done more than just read about these creatures. He captured those beauties because he laid in wait for them. When one fluttered by, he went after it with his net. Then he examined it in detail, identified it, and made it look its best. Afterwards he kept it ready for display. By analogy, illustrations will profit by similar treatment. Let us go step by step.

Watching for Them

Illustrations are everywhere. They flit before us as we read. They cluster in the garden; they line up in the market. Children dramatize them for us, and travel loads us with them. The newspaper often has an amazing ten cents worth of them. The Bible spills over with them. Your experience, mine, and theirs is a movie in technicolor.

The wise preacher will develop an eye for illustrations; E. W. Sangster called it the "trawling eye." This sight can be learned. Right now take pencil and paper and describe the appearance and feel of fifteen different fruits. Go on, do it. Makes you think, doesn't it? That's the whole idea.

Go after that which will illuminate the Word. Try to see what you look at, listen to, what you hear, and savor what you taste. A technique used by artists to make the world more appreciated is called framing. As the word implies, a frame selects a small part of a general scene, shuts out the rest, and magnifies the detail of the chosen section. Your preaching ministry is your frame: look at less and see more.

Victor Hugo penned this masterpiece describing a hideous seamonster:

It winds about its victim, covering him and enveloping him in its slimy folds. It is a spider in its shape, a chameleon in its rapid changes of hue. When angry it becomes purple. Its most disgusting characteristic is its impalpability. Its slimy folds strangle; its very touch paralyzes. It looks like a mass of scorbutic gangrened flesh: it is a hideous picture of loathsome disease. Once fixed, you cannot tear it away. It clings closely to its prey. How does it do so? By creating a vacuum.... It is a pneumatic machine that attacks you. You are struggling with a void which possesses eight antennae. No scratches, no bites, but an indescribable suffocation. This terrible wretch grins upon you by a thousand foul mouths. The hydra incorporates itself with the man, and the man with the hydra. You become one and the same. The hideous dream is in your bosom.

The devilfish draws you into its system. He drags you to him and into him; bound helplessly, glued where you stand, utterly powerless, you are gradually emptied into a loathsome receptable which is the monster himself.

Horrible isn't it? But brilliant. It may make you reach for the dictionary: that's one thing in its favor. Of course, a master is at work here. He forces you through a nightmare encounter with an octopus. Looking at it with a preacher's eye, however, you see the hideous repulsiveness of sin: it envelopes, it compels, it destroys.

Obviously we see either what we want or are trained to see. In the tense confusion of a road accident, the doctor looks for the injured and is aware of human needs; the policeman is concerned with the position of the vehicles and looks for telltale marks on the road; a passerby sees blood, and faints. Each sees what he is looking for.

Sometimes the *cryptic sentence* is an illustration. Take this one of B. Edinger: "Inside the will of God there is no failure; outside the will of God there is no success." That wraps up a big truth in a small parcel.

Analogies are useful too: they help us explain things by comparison. A pastor moved into a recently acquired parsonage. To his delight there were many fruit trees in the garden. Being a townsman, however, he had not learned the art of pruning; so he hired a gardener.

Noticing the pastor watching, the gardener paused. "These trees have not been properly pruned for years," he said. "You won't notice much difference in the quantity of fruit for about three years. Then you will see the result of my pruning. You'll have better fruit and more of it. This is what I call the long-term policy."

The pastor eyed him curiously and thought . . . "Now no chastening [pruning] for the present seemeth to be joyous, but grievous; nevertheless afterward. . . ." The long-term policy idea—afterward. He put it on ice and went back to the gardener-teacher.

"I'm being careful not to cut too much off this tree," he volunteered. "I don't want to give this tree too great a shock.

"Hold it," said the pastor to himself, and turned aside. "I didn't know a tree had feeling or could sustain shock." He looked with keener interest at the gardener. A sharp tool was in his leathery hand. He seemed to feel the suffering he was causing the tree and yet knew this was the only way to improve its fruitfulness. But he was careful not to inflict more pain than was necessary.

"I must get this," the pastor told himself. "It's just like God who 'will not suffer you to be tempted [tested, pruned] above that ye are able [to bear]. . . .'"

You can imagine the pastor went back for more—and got it—but that's another story. Unexpectedly, reasons for God's sometime strange ways with us had been illustrated by an analogy.

Allegories or parables are an aid in preaching and teaching. Jesus often used them. He made use of familiar objects and events.

A Scottish landowner who was unexpectedly detained while away from home, sent a postcard to his farm manager with instructions as follows: "Do try to get rid of the thistles. Be sure to deepen the ditches; they so easily get silted up. Mind the fences lest the lambs stray. It is time to plow up the big meadows. You may expect a visit from me very soon now." Try thinking over these instructions with the return of Christ in mind. The landowner evidently was a man of few words. He might have been even more concise and said simply, "Occupy till I come" (Luke 19:13). What splendid material is here to illustrate that command.

History teems with illustrative events. In the museum at Stanford University, California, is a large painting depicting the trials of an early pioneer family. It is titled "Crossing the Plains." Under the pitiless glare of the noonday sun the wagon has jogged to a pathetic standstill; the oxen are prostrate with thirst. A man of the family reluctantly drips water into a bowl—for the beasts. Three laps and it will be gone. The rest of the family cast weary eyes on what is happening.

A few paces away a pretty young daughter kneels in prayer—her face in her hands. Close by, crossed slats and a few bones are grim reminders that some never lived to see the land of their dreams. If these oxen perish, all hope is lost.

It is an anguished picture of hopes and fears, of uncertainty and dependence upon frail supports. It also searchingly asks, "What are your hopes for crossing the great divide between time and eternity?"

Or, for another historical allusion: Oliver Goldsmith in 1756, having obtained his medical doctor's degree, found himself penniless. He applied for a job in a naval hospital but was rejected. To earn himself a pittance, he pounded drugs. Utterly disappointed with life, he seized a pen and began to pour out his soul in a torrent of words, hoping to be published. Most of this was rejected, but the flow could not be damned. Afterwards, his work of this bleak period was acclaimed and became a classic: *The Vicar of Wakefield*. So often Christians find their disappointments are God's appointments.

Biography offers us rich veins of illustrative ore. G. Campbell Morgan relates that when conducting special meetings in the Midlands of England, numbers of people would go into the inquiry room after the sermon. Kneeling by one shabbily dressed man, the preacher discovered he was a ragpicker. He had grown old in the service of sin and Satan. His eyes became pools as the evangelist told him of the blood of Christ that cleanses from all sin. This was sufficient for him, and by faith he received Christ's forgiveness.

The next inquirer was the mayor of the city. Six weeks earlier he had sent the ragpicker to jail for a month's hard labor. But he had a personal spiritual need too, and the evangelist told him the same message. It proved sufficient for him. All men are equally needy at the Cross: "The poor man and the oppressor meet together; the Lord gives light to the eyes of both" (Proverbs 29:13, Amplified).

Here is another biographical gem.

> The indomitable missionary David Brainerd was burning to take the gospel to a ferocious tribe of Indians. One evening he pitched his tent near a settlement, resolving to enter it next day. To his surprise, the tribe gave him an almost reverential reception; he could not understand why.
>
> It was not until afterward that he learned that during his night's encampment a party of warriors had silently surrounded his tent, meaning to kill him. They looked in and saw him kneeling in prayer. They also saw a rattlesnake creeping to his side. Fascinated, they watched as it lifted its head to strike the missionary, fleck its forked tongue and then . . . glide away. The warriors huddled together, "The Great Spirit is with the paleface; let us go." The Shadow of the Almighty!

Don't miss the light that shines through windows like these.

Personal experience is an unfailing source of illustration. A child brought home his school report card showing satisfactory grades for everything except conduct. Mother queried the reason.

"Well, Mother," was the frank reply, "conduct is my most difficult subject." Just so, but it took a child to say it.

The author recently went into a public library. Shelves marked "Bible" caught his attention, so he went to browse. There may have been good reason, or the book may have been wrongly filed, but the first title he saw was *The Principle of the Fairy Tale*. Possibly equating Bible teachings with fairy tales accounts for the jungle-like conditions of society today.

We have now considered some areas in which we can find colorful illustrations. A complete differentiation of type is not possible—or necessary—but sufficient has been written to show the possibilities.

NETTING THEM

These butterflies will flutter by and be lost if you are not alert. Therefore, regard it as part of your work to make a note of an illustration when you see it.

Illustrations you read in your own books can be directly indexed in your card index, as previously explained. If you are reading a borrowed volume, the illustration must be transcribed into your book of illustrations and then indexed. To do this, give each illustration book a number—I-1, I-2, etc. This with the page number transferred to the appropriate section of your index will suffice.

Those you gather hour by hour from life's passing show must be jotted down in your loose-leaf note-book, ready for more ambitious treatment later. This takes time, of course, but so does planing wood.

SHAPING THEM

Your brief notes, to be of service, should be transferred to your illustration book. While doing this you should bring your preaching insights to bear upon them. You must shape them to your purpose. Take time doing this and make it an exercise in creative writing. Use live, luminous words. Don't be content with the first draft; revise and keep at it. Produce the best word pictures you can. Prune what you have written, especially if you are proud of it. Remember what Sir William Osler said, "It is often harder to boil down than to write." An artist is always sketching; a composer does endless studies; they want to perfect their art. So should you.

While enjoying a camping vacation in one of the beautiful western states, we were often entranced by constant changes of panorama. The highest mountain in the area seemed to diffuse a presidential aura over the entire scene. It enriched us with new thoughts of Christ. The following went into our illustration book:

Far Above All

From where we were camping, the noble snow-capped Mount Jefferson towered above the tree-clad slopes of the lesser heights. Mirrored in the still waters of Detroit Lake she reigned like a queen over the whole beautiful panorama— glorious, majestic.

It was at sundown, however, that we were treated to a breathtaking scene. As the great orb slowly sank below the tops of the western mountains, the lake slowly passed from twilight to shade, as if a blind were being drawn. Campers shivered and threw extra logs on their fires. Imperceptibly, soft shadows crept up the eastern slope of the mountain: trees turned from green to dark blue to black. Sounds were muffled as the blanket of darkness gently tucked us in.

But high above the shadows and with silvery peak still bathed in a pink glow, Jefferson seemed not to rise from earth but, like the New Jerusalem, to descend from God out of heaven.

To see it like this was to be suffused with worship and

wonder. It stood alone, enhanced by its solitary splendor, eminent over every other peak . . . reflecting the light of another world.

Behold, then, Jesus; the Son of God, yet Son of Man; risen in triumph, ascended in glory; most illustrious. When He is compared with earth's brightest lights, they are as shadows of the night. Supreme . . . all-glorious.

"Brightness of the Father's glory,
Sunshine of the Father's face. . . ." image of the invisible God . . . the first born of all creation.

Inspired and lifted by the rapture of this holy moment, we whispered in worship, "O come, let us adore *Him*, Christ the Lord."

You may want some of your illustrations years after they have been in pickle. This means details will have become blurred. How glad you will be you painted the best word picture you could and that you have it immediately available.

Using Them

It is a happy, though rare experience, when illustrations ring your doorbell, so to speak, just when you need them. Normally, in preparing to preach—as in preparing to write—every thought is drawn from a vast personal reservoir stocked by observation, memory, imagination, reading, and deduction. It is gratifying to the preacher when he is able quickly to find an appropriate illustration. Recording and indexing are worthwhile chores.

There is no rule for the number of illustrations to be used in one sermon. Some messages, structured on pictorial Bible events and stories, need no other illustration. Some do best with one and others benefit by one in each main division of the discourse.

Keep to facts; acknowledge sources; remember, illustration is not argument. Don't use an illustration if it is only doubtfully relevant. Give old chestnuts a ten-year vacation.

8

MESSAGE

Sermons may be considered in two obvious categories. There is the sermon directed specifically to the unbeliever, to show him his great need of God and the way to Him through Christ. The lucid preaching of the gospel indicates the *evangelistic* sermon.

In the second category are the messages prepared for those who have received Christ as Saviour and Lord and are now learning of Him: the Christians. These folk need all the help they can get from their minister. Their birth into the kingdom of God was supernaturally by the Word of God (1 Peter 1:23), and their growth towards maturity is by the same means (Hebrews 5:14). They need regular, challenging ministry of the Word.

While some messages may aim at two objectives, it would seem advisable, normally, to make the full thrust at a single target.

It is not desirable to make rigid distinctions between the various types of sermons for believers. However, for the purpose of examination here, it is useful to consider four.

First is the *devotional* sermon which, in the main, is to encourage believers to move on with God. It is a faith builder: it may deal with Christian know-how. Pagan philosophies swirl round the Christian and the Church; it is vital to affirm and strengthen our confidence in God and His Word. It is also necessary to caution Christians against the subtle erosion of this godless age and to implant and cultivate longings after righteousness and true holiness. These are the thrusts of the devotional sermon.

Then there is the message with strong *ethical content*. A profession—the law, for instance—has standards of conduct for its members. Ethical teaching, the standard for Christians, forms a big stratum of Bible truth. Secular philosophies issue in a certain related way of living. Carl F. H. Henry in writing about naturalism, for example, says it has these tenets: (a) The ultimate reality is nature; (b) Man is essentially an animal; (c) Truth and right are time-bound and changing.* The ethical results of these beliefs are clearly apparent today, yet they can be understood because they *are* a result of them.

Judaeo-Christian ethics start with God: "Hear, O Israel; the Lord our God is one Lord: and thou shalt love the Lord thy God with all thy heart, and with all thy soul, and with all thy mind, and with all thy strength" (Mark 12:29, 30). Man's first duty, therefore, is the worship of God and the acceptance of His supremacy in every area of his life. Such worship issues in neighbor-love as a necessity of the moral life: "Thou shalt love thy neighbor as thyself" (Mark 12:31).

In addition to the Ten Commandments, the Bible contains much guidance for our ethical routing. Its principles are not subject to any change by time, place, or society. Therefore, it is important that the Christian's

*Carl F. H. Henry, Christian Personal Ethics (Grand Rapids, Mich.: William B. Eerdmans Publishing Company, 1957).

inner motivation be activated and strengthened by solid ministry from the Word along ethical lines.

There is also the *interpretative sermon*. In one sense, of course, all our sermons should have this quality. It is wise to work on the assumption that most people know very little about the Bible: explanation is always needed. "Lack of knowledge," it has been candidly said, "is a prominent and pervading defect of personal Christianity, to remove with instruction is the only means." The interpretative sermon, however, will deal with professedly difficult passages of the Word and explain them. A series of messages based on one of the Bible books would perhaps show this method at its best.

The *apologetic sermon* offers proofs for Christian belief. It is true the Christian faith needs no defense, but its followers need to know how to defend what they believe they believe.

The fourth broad division includes messages for special functions or on particular subjects: the *occasional sermon*.

The Bible's message is for everyone: it is relevant to every need. The preacher, therefore, needs a sensitive spirit at all times to catch the whisper of God and discern the hidden need of his people. Only then will he bring the right message at the right time. Deepening acquaintance with God in the secret place and heart contact with his people, preferably in their homes, are ways to develop this awareness.

The preacher-to-be must not despise or neglect the practice of making sermon outlines; neither must he regard this as unspiritual. Doesn't the Bible encourage us to "seek that ye may excel to the edifying of the church"? (1 Corinthians 14:12).

A simple practice learned in Bible school days was known as "Looking for Seven Chief Lessons." Each week students were required to select a special passage from their assigned Bible reading and draw from it seven important lessons. Whether or not this material was ever used, they had to seek out and list these lessons week by week.

Suppose Luke 5, verses 2 through 11 had been your selection. The story centers on Simon Peter, discouraged because of a wasted night, hesitant to obey Jesus' command, complying reluctantly—then hauling in a great catch of fish. Going through the passage step by step, we might come up with something like this:

How Fullness Can Follow Failure
Luke 5:1-11

1. Lend Jesus your vessel	verse 3
2. Listen to Jesus' voice	verse 4
3. Leave the past behind	verse 5a
4. Learn to obey	verse 5b
5. Look for the miraculous	verse 6
6. Link up with others like-minded	verse 7
7. Love the Lord wholeheartedly	verses 9, 11

Thirty minutes practice like this each day may sound tedious, but it will soon become fascinating. It will loosen up your mental joints. Enthusiastic piano players with their eye on musical success devote hours to strengthening one weak finger or perfecting a run. Should a minister be any less dedicated? Simple practice, as explained above, can start you digging below the surface of the Scripture.

A sermon needs *depth*. People have deep needs and—surprisingly, perhaps—deep thoughts at times. If they don't, they need to be challenged to venture beyond their depth. Our lighter conscious thoughts are like the twigs, dust and oil meandering along the surface of a stream, but below there are levels with strong currents. Christians need to have God's Word search them at deepening levels. If the preacher is not scratching them where they itch, perhaps they will begin to itch where scratched—by the Word—in a more needful area. There is a lot of sense in the saying that the preacher is to comfort the afflicted and afflict the comfortable. We may understand, but we cannot condone the hard-working woman who came to a service and confided: "Yes, it is such a rest after a hard week's work to just sit down and not think about anything."

The preacher's studying needs to be at deepening levels. Meditation is a mental activity that deepens you. It makes you tunnel beneath life's clichés and easy explanations. It is not necessary a pastor should pass on all he discovers, but he needs to keep ahead of his congregation; and not for this reason alone, for if we are not deepening our mental ditches, we are in a rut.

Good sermons come from the depths of a man's experience.

> The sermons of Augustine are strong in the elements of experience, witness-bearing, dialectic, and practical application; they are less affected by secular training and more infused with the gospel; they give the impression of being by a man who has triumphed over the flesh, false philosophy, heathendom and heresy, who spoke from the depths of his own experience. They show the gifts of keen understanding, a power of deep speculation, precise expression, wide powers of illustration and a deep sense of what salvation means.*

A sermon is entitled to *dignity*. Dr. E. W. Sangster has given the sermon its right elevation by contrasting it with an address. "An address," he says, "is a man talking to men. A sermon is a man speaking from God." So be it— always. Keep your pulpit work dignified, brother. If we want the circus, we'll go there; but in the pulpit . . . speak "as the oracles of God . . . that God in all things may be glorified through Jesus Christ, to whom be praise and dominion for ever and ever" (1 Peter 4:11).

This means, among other things, giving it distinction

---

*Philip Schaff and Joann Hertzog, *The New Schaff-Hertzog Encyclopedia of Religious Knowledge,* article on "Preaching" (Grand Rapids, Mich.: Baker Book House).

both in treatment and presentation. A subject becomes edifying according to its handling by the preacher.

A sermon must have *dynamics*. Prayer in the study is imperative. The Holy Spirit guides and inspires a minister, not only in the solemn moments of utterance but in the quiet hours of preparation. These two—prayer and preparation—like reciprocating piston rods, transmit the power.

We shall now consider different ways in which God's Word *hooks* us. Examples given may provoke ideas; let them stimulate practice.

Sometimes a *single word* flashes like a neon sign. Instantly, by the law of association, its occurence in another setting will pop up in your mind, then another, and another from the background of your Scripture knowledge. Jot these down at once, especially if it is not your purpose to study them immediately. The concordance can later be checked for other appearances of the word.

Ponder again the incident in Luke 5; the story seems to pivot on the "nevertheless" in verse 5. "Master," protested Simon Peter, an experienced fisherman, "we have toiled all the night, and have taken nothing." Doubt and despondency were freezing him on the inside; it was touch and go. He might just miss a net-breaking catch of fish. Then the warm power of Christ's command thawed him, the discouragement floated away, and he agreed to let down the net. "Nevertheless" marked the turning point.

Other occurences of this word show, similarly, its tensile quality. It functions as a shock absorber to cushion the bumps of life, as the context will show. We might call the subject:

TENSIONS

1. Tensions through discouragement	Luke 5:5
2. Tensions through delay	John 11:15
3. Tensions through discipline	Hebrews 12:11
4. Tensions through sorrow	John 16:6, 7
5. Tensions through preaching	2 Timothy 1:12

In each case you will notice a threatening thrust is met by a divine counterthrust. The point of impact is at the word "nevertheless." In this and similar cases a keyword will unlock several doors.

Sometimes a *phrase* will trigger your thinking. "Till He come," marks the turning point in affairs at the Lord's second advent. At that critical moment certain events are due to stop and others begin. It will be the Christian's zero hour. What will happen?

ZERO HOUR
"Till He come."

1. Certain things will finish
   Our celebration of the Lord's Supper: 1 Corinthians 11:26
   Our probation as the Lord's stewards: Luke 19:13
   Our temptation as the Lord's subjects: Luke 22:28
   Our separation as the Lord's beloved: 1 Peter 1:8
   Our limitation as God's children: Romans 8:23
   Our humiliation as heaven's citizens: Philippians 3:20
   Our consternation as Jesus' disciples: John 21:12
2. Certain things will then begin
   The Memorial Supper will give place to the Marriage Supper: Matthew 26:29; Revelation 19:5-9
   Probation will give way to jubilation: Matthew 25:21
   Temptation will be exchanged for coronation: Luke 22:28-30
   Separation will terminate in mobilization: Romans 8:19, 21, 23
   Humiliation will end in glorification: Philippians 3:21
   Consternation will receive its explanation: 1 Corinthians 13:12

Here are the bones of a teaching sermon, or probably several. You have a comprehensive plan for further study and development.

A *verse*—or part of a verse—often crystallizes a certain aspect of truth. As an example, take Paul's well-known vote of confidence in God given not when he was cresting the wave of success and popularity, but in jail, suffering afflictions for the sake of the gospel: "I know whom I have believed, and am persuaded that he is able to keep that which I have committed unto him against that day"

(2 Timothy 1:12). This is the serene statement of a stable servant of Christ.

By using personal pronouns, Paul is saying, "Look at me." Against the dark background of imprisonment and isolation flashes the picture of a mature Christian. Let us approach the verse from that angle:

PICTURE OF A CHRISTIAN MAN

1. A prepared Man: *ready against that day*
2. A committed Man: *committed unto Him*
3. An assured Man: *He is able to keep*
4. A positive Man: *I know*
5. A confident Man: *Whom I have believed*

You may not care to have these facets of Paul's belief set out in this way; they may even irritate you. But perhaps as with an oyster, the irritation will cause you to produce a pearl of your own.

A *paragraph* or more will at times organize itself round a leading thought or subject. In Matthew 2:1, we read of "wise men from the east" who came to Jerusalem to search for the Christ. Their understanding of astrology, no doubt, explains why they were called wise, but their wisdom is seen in other directions.

WISE MEN

They were wise because:
1. They took notice of something unusual:
   His star in the east: verse 2
2. They went in search of Christ: *Where is He?* verse 2
3. Worship, not curiosity, was their motive: *Come to worship Him:* verse 2
4. They listened to instruction from the Scriptures:
   It is written by the prophet: verse 5
5. They offered Christ the best they had:
   —they fell down and worshiped Him.
   —they opened their treasures.
   —They presented unto Him gifts: verse 11
6. They departed another way: verse 12
   Always happens when people truly worship

This could be improved, but even as it is you can see the possibility of an evangelistic Christmas message. However, it would need to lay in *your* mental incubator for a while.

A chapter usually contains several paragraphs—more material than can be used in one sermon. But you can spotlight a dominant line of truth as you see it in the passage. In the first chapter of First Samuel, for instance, you could select all the material relevant to Hannah and facet the testing and triumph of this noble woman. Or *prayer* might be your central subject—from the same chapter—where several of its avenues are illustrated.

Suppose, however, that on reading the chapter for the nth time you are arrested by the significance of the *house of the Lord*. This story of family life brings it clearly into focus. As a pastor, you are an overseer of a house of the Lord in your city. Your congregation is made up of families, each with their share of problems. So you set about separating appropriate material from the rest of the chapter.

Every Christian should have a house of the Lord to which he should belong; but what should he expect of such an association? Let us see.

THE HOUSE OF THE LORD IN SHILOH

What did it provide for Hannah and Elkanah?
What does it offer me?
What should I expect when I attend?
1. A place of spiritual enlargement: verse 3
   —up out of the city: leaving daily life aside
   —to worship: could have done this at home,
      maybe, but special command: cf Hebrews 10:25
   —to sacrifice: praise, thanksgiving
2. A place to come with our sorrows: verse 7
   —discord in the home: verse 6
   —no children for Hannah: verse 2
3. A place where we can pray and wait
   —bitterness drained off: verse 10

—she *continued* praying: verse 12
4. A place for receiving counsel from a man of God:
   verses 13-18
   —talking it over
   —receiving help, spiritually, and physically
5. A place for the making of vows: verse 11
   marriage, for example
6. A place where we can bring our young: verse 24
   —to dedicate
   —later, for instruction
7. A place to return with thanksgiving: verse 24
   —as punctual with our praises as with petitions

These leading thoughts have come from the Bible passage; they are therein illustrated and so constitute the basis of an exposition. "Expository preaching," declared Donald Barnhouse, "is the act of explaining the text of the Word of God, using all the experiences of life and learning to illustrate the exposition."

Enough has now been written to show how ideas can explode during our daily reading of the Bible. The mind has its muscles; they can be trained to work better by daily practice. If they are not exercised, they will become weak and flabby.

Because of the knowledge explosion of the past quarter century, we may feel our minds are stretched much more than those of people who lived say in the seventeenth century. This may be true of certain areas of knowledge, but what congregation today could take Matthew Henry's preaching method and plan?

At his 9 a.m. service he would preach for an hour from the Old Testament—each chapter in sequence. At 3 p.m. he would do the same with the New Testament. In October, 1692, at his midweek service, he started a series on "The Questions of the Bible." The first was, "Where art thou?" He concluded the series with, "What city is like unto the great City?" This was *twenty years later.*

To bring his people such a diet, this man gave himself devotedly to prayer and the ministry of the Word. He may have affected relatively few people according to our human way of calculation, but he did his duty as a minister of the Word. Of course, thousands of ministers since those days have been glad to drink at the fountain of *Matthew Henry's Commentary*, "which," said Spurgeon, "every minister ought to read . . . entirely and carefully through, once, at least. I should recommend you," he goes on, "to get through it in the next twelve months after you leave college. Begin at the beginning, and resolve that you will traverse the good land from Dan to Beersheba. You will acquire a vast store of sermons if you read with your notebook close at hand; and as for thoughts, they will swarm around you like twittering swallows around an old gable towards the close of autumn."

We may not advocate this regimen today, but we will have to admit "there were giants in those days."

It is pertinent to our subject to inquire how a man with such a preaching schedule could find time to write such a monumental commentary. We quote his own words:

> If any desire to know how so mean and obscure a person as I am, who in learning, judgment, felicity of expression, and all advantages for such a service, am less than the least of all my Master's servants, come to venture upon so great a work, I can give no other account of it but this.
>
> It has long been my practice, what little time I had to spare in my study from my constant preparations for the pulpit, to spend it in drawing up expositions upon some parts of the New Testament, not so much for my own use, as partly for my own entertainment, because I know not how to employ my thoughts and time more to my satisfaction.

This man, so humble in his own estimation, finds first place in Spurgeon's gallery of commentators.

He is most precious and pithy, sound and sensible, suggestive and sober, terse and trustworthy, You will find him to be glittering with metaphors, rich in analogies, overflowing with illustrations, superabundant in reflections. He delights in apposition and alliteration; he is usually plain, quaint and full of pith; he sees right through a text directly; apparently he is not critical, but he quietly gives the result of an accurate critical knowledge of the original fully up to the best critics of his time.

These rather long references to Henry have been made not so much to boost his commentary as to show the reflection of a man whose whole life was given to preaching, teaching, and writing God's Word. It was his business, his life. Should it not also be ours?

Master Plan

Some, as the supreme truth on which to concentrate today, urge the simple Gospel; others, the cross; others, the fundamentals; others, reunion; others, foreign missions; others, holiness; others, the Second Coming; others, the Jew: so long as they press each golden truth we are utterly with them; but the moment they press their special truth *alone,* we are utterly opposed. Each truth is but one loaf; scatter, like Elisha, the twenty loaves: God never gave 66 books if less than 66 books would have done. There is no truth of God for which He has not made an ear somewhere. It takes the whole Book of God to counter the whole strategy of hell; and every error has its counter-truth in the Book.

—D. M. Panton
Bread for God's People

9
MASTER PLAN

A preacher's education never finishes. Life is a seminary; graduation will not come until he finishes his earthly course. What a man brings forth in his sermons reflects what he is and what he has learned. He is privileged to stand on the shoulders of the past.

Earlier chapters of this book have shown the high points and the great significance of *permanent preparation* —long-term and continuing. This cannot be too strongly emphasized. The minister you so much admire today is the product of his earlier years. As a broad river begins with a trickle far away, so does a man's ministry commence in the obscure hills of the past.

Consider these injunctions to a young minister: "Take time and trouble to keep yourself spiritually fit. Bodily fitness has a certain value, but spiritual fitness is essential, both for the present life and for the life to come." Spiritual calisthenics will develop stamina and the beauty of holiness. (Greek: *kallos*—beauty; and *sthenos*—strength.) Take time and trouble. . . .

The injunctions continue: "It is because we realize the

paramount importance of the spiritual that we labor and struggle. . . . See that [people] look up to you because you are an example to them in your speech and behavior, in your love and faith and sincerity. Concentrate . . . on your reading and on your preaching and teaching. . . . Give your whole attention, all your energies, to these things, so that your progress is plain for all to see. Keep a critical eye both upon your own life and on the teaching you give, and if you continue to follow the line . . . indicated you will not only save your soul but the souls of many of your hearers as well" (1 Timothy 4, Phillips). These demanding words burn with seriousness: they should be branded on every minister's heart—if not engraven on the wall of his study.

We turn now to the work of preparing a specific sermon. Dr. W. M. Taylor defines homiletics as "the science which treats of the analysis, classification, preparation, composing, and delivery of sermons viewed as addressed to the popular mind on subjects suggested by the Word of God and designed for the conversion of sinners and the edification of believers." In this definition, homiletics is called a science; others term it an art or a craft. We will not quarrel with these technicalities. It is sufficient if we fully understand that preaching is a skill and not the resort of a man who is no good for anything else.

Austin Phelps' definition of a sermon points up certain differences. Enumerating his points for clarity, we have:

A SERMON IS

1. An oral address
2. To the popular mind
3. Upon religious truth
4. As contained in the Christian Scriptures
5. And elaborately treated
6. With a view to persuasion.

It will be observed that more is expected of a sermon

than a little weak thought mixed with water and served cold. Preachers who forsake their study and depend on the inspiration of the moment don't usually get it. They may, indeed, have all the confidence of a clergyman who boasted, "Often, when I'm in the vestry, I do not know what I am going to talk about; but I go into the pulpit and preach and think nothing of it."

His bishop hearing this promptly informed him, "And you are quite right in thinking nothing of it, for your church wardens have told me they share your opinion."

Because the message entrusted to us is so important we should spare no pains in becoming skilled in the craft of presenting it. Writers spend hours learning the principles of their art; then by constant practice and revision they produce acceptable articles or stories. Persevering they look upon rejection slips not as evidence of their inability but as necessary steps towards their goal. Seeking to excel—this must be the dynamic attitude of the preacher.

A sermon is a structure. It must be put together with care. This is the purpose of homiletical training. To be stable a structure must have *unity:* that is, it must be complete in itself; the arrangement of its parts must produce a single harmonious design.

Then it must have *coherence,* or the quality of being logical, consistent, intelligible. In the realm of literature, a reader will lose all interest in a story that lacks coherence.

Finally, a structure must have *proportion* in the relation of its parts to the whole. This produces balance and symmetry.

Stating these requirements may perhaps seem to burden the subject unnecessarily. "If my heart is burning with a message," some may say, "do I have to bother about unity, coherence, and proportion?" The answer is "No, not if you have already learned their importance." You have probably forgotten your schooling in English grammar, but you certainly—though, maybe, unconscious-ly—make use of its principles, even when swept to heights of eloquence.

> Inevitably there are some technicalities in our craft. We do not burden our congregations with them in any obvious way, though we serve our people the more effectively because we have made this technique the object of our close attention. Nor do we desire to detain in our company in this study the man to whom it all seems much ado about nothing. If he tells us that he has been preaching for forty years and knows nothing about all this, we may be tempted to tell him that we have often suspected so much and wished he had known a little more. For ourselves, we are determined to be workmen who need not to be ashamed.°

It is an unusual preacher, indeed, who does not snap up a new book on preaching. Most of us keep on reading —hoping, trusting to learn how to preach before we are called home.

Homiletics is the preacher's craft. Its study will teach him to focus and frame his thoughts when in the throes of preparation. It will give him courage to reject the super-fluous. It will assist him to think logically. His listeners will feel sure he has found a path through the wood and will follow him mentally step by step.

For ministry to either Christians or non-Christians, the most generally useful preaching is expository. We go to the Word of God reverently to find out what He intends us to know. Coming before the people, we then . . .

Interpret

Apply

Appeal

We interpret the meaning of the Bible passage, as we have seen it. We apply the teaching of the passage—its unchanging principles—to the contemporary situation

---

°W. E. Sangster, *The Craft of Sermon Construction* (London: The Epworth Press, 1949).

and need of people. We appeal—on the basis of this Bible truth—for the consent and cooperation of the will of our hearers.

This is preaching from the Bible *par excellence.* That it is to be the preacher's main work may seem obvious, as may the assumption that skills for this are taught in Bible colleges and seminaries. But Dr. A. W. Blackwood maintains that "with few exceptions, the young men in our theological seminaries wish they could learn how to preach from the Bible."*

When we go to the divine Word we are not to read into a text what *we* choose; we are to draw from it what God intends us to know. There may be some excuse for trying to find a verse that seems to say what we feel or want it to say, but this is rather like buying fruit to tie on a tree. To use a text of Scripture as a launching pad into a personally chosen orbit of unrelated thoughts—so as to impart a religious flavor—should be considered inexcusable: a form of ethical bunco.

Bible exposition, we repeat, is the preacher's main business. In this we must seek to excel whether our presentation of the day be by means of a word, a phrase, a verse, paragraph, chapter, or theme. If we become expository preachers, we shall never run dry. "Certainly, if you preach your own theories and ideas using Scripture texts merely as pegs to hang them on," writes Dr. J. S. Stewart, "you will soon be at the end of your resources—and the sooner the better. But if you will let the Scriptures speak their own message, if you will realize that every passage or text has its own quite distinctive meaning, you will begin to feel that the problem is not lack of fresh material, but the very embarrassment of riches, and with the Psalmist you will cry 'I rejoice at Thy Word as one that findeth great spoil.' "

---

*Andrew W. Blackwood, *Preaching from the Bible* (Nashville: Abingdon Press, 1941).

It is tragically apparent that substitutes are offered for this preaching from the Bible. David Womack writes:

> We are suffering today under a steady barrage of non-Biblical preaching. Far too many pastors of our generation have taken their methods and their content from modern advertising, popular psychology, and public relations. They offer us gimmicks rather than gospel, entertainment rather than involvement. Their gimmicks catch and hold our interest much as a dragged string catches the eye of a kitten. The kitten is intrigued by the string and may even leap into action in an attempt to capture his false prey, but he fails to find anything on which to feed when he wins the prize.

Topical addresses have eye-catching appeal—but there is also danger here. It is easy to jump at a Scripture passage that appears to be related to an event of the day and, dogmatically, declaim thus and so. But in so doing, basic laws of interpretation can be broken, the Bible can be handled deceitfully, and the minds of the people can be violated. If a preacher uses the topical approach, he must be alert to the possible abuse of this method. Let all such preachers be cautioned by noting Paul's enlightened attitude. "We are not," he says, "like so many (as hucksters, tavern keepers, making trade of) peddling God's Word—short-measuring and adulterating the divine message; but as [men] of sincerity *and* the purest motive, commissioned *and* sent by God, we speak [His message] in Christ, the Messiah, in the [very] sight *and* Presence of God" (2 Corinthians 2:17, Amplified). These words are not too strong.

Now and again the pew expresses its dissatisfaction with the pulpit, as in the following letter from a reader of *Christianity Today* (December 8, 1967):

> For the past forty years I have been puzzled by one characteristic of the usual sermon. . . . We enter the church building for our religious service. The sanctuary is adorned . . . to put us in the proper frame of mind for worship. Religious symbols meet our eyes. Music is being played to evoke

an emotional response. We sing a hymn. There is prayer, Scripture reading, and often special choir music.

Then, when we have carefully been brought to a peak and are ready to respond to a discourse concerning the Deity—the preacher arises and makes a crack about baseball. Or it might be about football, motoring or television, but it is guaranteed to put us back to where we were on Saturday night. . . .

The opening sentence follows the pattern of the commercial that comes in the middle of a baseball or football game. But let us be logical. The situation is different. During the break for the commercial, the audience tunes out mentally and heads for the refrigerator. Their minds must be caught and held. . . . The preacher's congregation is not in front of the refrigerator with their mouths full of fried chicken. They are seated in the pews where they can't get away without violating the mores of two thousand years. Instead of being let down for the commercial, they have been built up for the sermon.

So, please preacher, spare us the letdown.*

Preaching which repeats pious commonplaces and platitudes for the sake of a response from those who would rather hear these than think is not preaching from the Bible. The Bible challenges our thinking and blasts our mediocrity. Often, it says what we don't like— but certainly need—to hear. Preaching that is simply concerned with stirring emotions and that's all, fails because it does not penetrate to the will—where decisions are made. Its results are assessed by feelings—alone. It produces people who live on their feelings: they rise and fall with their moods. For these people, Christianity in general and the church in particular succeeds or fails according to their subjective condition. A course of preaching from the Bible would do them a power of good. It would reorient them so that God—and not they—would be at the center of the universe. They would learn that their personal feelings do not put God out of existence

---

* *Christianity Today*, December 8, 1967.

or jeopardize His throne of government. They would discover that God is more concerned with our character than our comfort and that adversities are not there to be avoided but accepted and exploited for good by God's unfailing grace.

By this time some of the mystery surrounding expository preaching may have been dispelled; but there are still further misconceptions needing correction.

Expository preaching is not giving a word by word commentary on a certain verse or passage of Scripture. Such detailed word examination may be necessary in the study but not its reiteration in the pulpit. The expository sermon has structure.

It is not expressing random thoughts about a verse or verses. This may have its place in a prayer group to give encouragement for intercession.

It is not a Sunday school lesson-type discussion where any student can make an observation.

It is not a collection of verses scattered throughout the Bible but joined by a common theme—unless it is a structured unity.

It is not a multicommentary hamburger.

Expository preaching has reference to the way a passage is handled, first in preparation and then in preaching. With acknowledgement to Farris D. Whitesell the following are some of the components of expository preaching:

1. The Bible passage chosen (word, verse or verses, paragraph, chapter, or Book) is treated as one complete unit.
2. The primary, central meaning of that passage is sought out and thoughtfully weighed.
3. Its relation to the immediate context is carefully considered.
4. The age-abiding truth and principles of the passage are gathered.
5. These truths are arranged around the one central theme of the passage in balanced proportion.

6. Simplification, illustration, and argument are used to apply the central truth to the hearers.

7. Sometimes by intellectual appeal, at others through the emotions, a challenge is presented to the will (heart) of the hearers. A verdict is called for.*

We will now show some of the values of this type of preaching.

1. *It helps the preacher to treat the Bible impartially.* Expository preaching is at its best when it proceeds steadily through a Bible book. This keeps the preacher from gravitating too often to easier or more familiar passages. Steady progress of this kind usually is appreciated by thoughtful parishioners.

2. *It enables the preacher to treat the Scripture fairly.* It becomes his duty to find out and show what is the major theme in the passage, while the context restrains him from making wild deductions or drawing unbalanced conclusions. Because he is living with that section of the Bible, his thinking is modified by the knowledge accumulated.

3. *It saves the preacher from becoming monotonous or riding a hobby horse.* A preacher may have his pet themes; but if he is a pastor ministering regularly to a constant nucleus of people, he and they need variety. Different subjects will be dealt with as and when the Bible presents them. Quite often this means that a coming problem is anticipated and dealt with before it has cut its first teeth. Later, because of emotional involvement, it would not be so easily handled.

During a period of six months a pastor worked through fifteen chapters of Genesis on Sunday mornings. In that time the following subjects came up for treatment:

Family religion

Temptation, repentance, and restoration

*Farris D. Whitesell, *Power in Expository Preaching* (Old Tappan, N. J.: Fleming H. Revell Co., 1963).

The conflict between flesh and spirit
The restoration of an erring brother
The tithe
The cause and cure of spiritual despondency
How God's Covenant is offered, established,
and fulfilled
Patience as a faith builder
The richness of some of God's titles
The meaning of separation
Walking before God
Courtesy and hospitality
The nurture of children
The ministry of intercession
The certainty of divine judgment
The bride of Christ

It will be seen that a practical and interesting spectrum of subjects was offered. Moreover, most of the preaching was related to three or four great Bible characters so illustrations abounded.

4. *It utilizes the interest of continuity.* For the more responsible hearers in the congregation, this means an added blessing. They come to realize the direction their preacher is taking and their appetites are whetted for the next installment. Such steady progress is satisfying, for "the plans of the mind *and* orderly thinking belong to man" (Proverbs 16:1, Amplified).

It will be surprising if members of the congregation will not enjoy personally reading their Bibles ahead of the coming Sunday. If they have difficulty in understanding it here and there, so much the better; they will be all ears at sermon time.

5. *It enables a minister to fulfill his commission to preach the Word.* He comes to his pulpit to declare honestly what God has said to him, and this is more important than a few personal opinions. To be able to

have this confidence he has labored in the Word and doctrine and is ready to interpret the timeless message of the passage. Authenticity and authority are the hallmarks of such preaching because it is Bible originated, supported, and propelled.

6. *It fulfills an educating process for preacher and people.* It offers a method of indoctrination that is interesting and persuasive. A former denominational president wrote these penetrating remarks in *Christianity Today:*

> During my ministry to my first two churches, I floundered. For ten years I searched for a way to make my sermons meaningful. I used both topical and exegetical preaching, but something was lacking. A very basic question had not been answered: What was my prime responsibility as a preacher?
> Then it dawned upon me that I was essentially a communicator of God's written Word, the Bible. This introduced a complete change in my approach to preaching. I was determined that when I left a church, the members would have a deposit of the Scriptures in their minds and an application of these sacred truths to their living. Somehow I would communicate an extensive and an intensive knowledge of the Bible. And this would have to be done at the 11 o'clock service on Sunday morning, when the most biblical illiterates were present.

The fruit of such preaching will be seen not only evangelistically, but ethically too. Full fruit is the objective.

7. *Expository preaching is both emotionally and intellectually satisfying.* Under the unction of the Holy Spirit, the expository sermon mounts in power because God has promised to bless His Word. As the Bible's sometimes involved statements are elucidated, its difficulties explained, its ancient truths made relevant, wandering thoughts are captured, hearts begin to quicken with joy, and hungry, inquiring minds are satisfied and

exercised. "A faithful ambassador is health" (Proverbs 13:17).

8. *It demands time, but it saves time.* Faris D. Whitesell writes: "Homiletical authorities commonly agree that the expository is the hardest type of preaching and that it usually requires more time in preparation." This is true, but we repeat the question previously asked in these pages: Why is a preacher freed from following a secular occupation? The answer is basic: so that he may give himself to prayer and the ministry of the Word. There is no shortcut to worthwhile preaching. The preacher who does not give his time to his preparation is acting under false pretenses.

On the other hand, the expository preacher is usually saved from the uncertainty of not knowing what to preach about. He does not have to spend time turning the pages of the Bible hoping to drop on a text or subject. He can get right down to his study and the construction of his outline. The outline, says Dr. G. Campbell Morgan, that prince of expositors, is more important than the writing of the sermon.

To a consideration of some different types of expository outlines, we now turn our attention.

Method

"God is not the Author of confusion but of order." Form is the embodiment and expression of order. It is a scientific term conveying the idea of a fixed model, a definite pattern, with certain dimensions and proportions in accordance with a plan and a purpose. Form is therefore necessarily both inclusive and exclusive, embracing all that is essential to completeness, excluding all that is superfluous. To discover the Divine Builder's design explains both what is present and what is absent, and interprets the meaning of every part.

—A. T. Pierson
Knowing the Scriptures

10
METHOD

Part I

It is important in our pulpit work that we keep from becoming stereotyped. We need variety, not only of subject but in presentation too. In other words, as when thinking of building a house, we should give consideration to different floor plans.

"The power of a sermon," says Halford E. Lucock, "lies in its structure, not in its decoration." This axiom is fully supported by the pulpit masters. Building the structure is where the finest skills of our craft are evidenced.

The labels we shall use in this and the following chapter belong to the study, not the pulpit. They are simply to help us in our practice. Facility with scales and arpeggios is utterly essential in the studio—for the piano student. However, these exercises are not heard, as such, on the concert platform, though they make possible a finished performance as nothing else will.

The Analytical Method

This is a good way to handle a long or involved text.

It consists of finding and examining separately, the central thought in each segment of the text, then in close relation to the main truth of the whole.

Paul in his Epistles is celebrated for his involved statements. It is to be feared he would not have much acceptance as a magazine writer today: his sentences are too long. One, for instance, in Ephesians 4:11-16, in the King James Version, contains 163 words. Today's average length for popular reading is about 17. This could well be why many contemporary readers think the Bible is dull and passé. They miss a great deal because they lack the patience to examine Bible statements closely. The helpfulness of a modern translation can be understood at this point; that of J. B. Phillips expresses the passage mentioned in five separate sentences. This helps.

Suppose you have decided to preach from part of this involved Pauline sentence, using one of its major themes as follows:

> Grow up into Him in all things, which is the head, even Christ: from whom the whole body fitly joined together and compacted by that which every joint supplieth, according to the effectual working in the measure of every part, maketh increase of the body unto the edifying of itself in love. (verses 15, 16.)

The complexity of this short section leaves you almost breathless, doesn't it? But now looking at the passage again, you will conclude that the first few words form the key—*grow up into Him*. The remainder of the passage explains how this growth will come about or *maketh increase*.

The context shows that Paul is writing about the Church Universal, the Body of Christ; so, *growing up into Him* refers to the growth of the Body of Christ as a whole. Now, the local church is a miniature of the Body of Christ (or is intended to be) so must be included in our consideration.

The central idea, then, is the growth of the Church. This is simple, so far. But now we have some complicated language to unravel. We must wrestle with this until it becomes simplified in our thinking; then we shall be able to explain it to the congregation.

First, let us try to analyze it by disjointing it and writing it down thus:

Central truth: Grow up into Him
Supporting truths:
1. . . . even Christ from whom. . . .
2. the whole body fitly joined together . . .
3. compacted by that which every joint supplieth. . . .
4. according to the effectual working in the measure of every part. . . .
5. maketh increase of the body unto the edifying of itself in love.

Here we have a central truth (unity) with five scriptural supporting truths (coherence), in balance (proportion). Our structure is beginning: we are digging the foundations.

Now we begin to analyze each of the sections, 1-5. It would help us, we think, if we knew more clearly what sections 3, 4, and 5 really mean. So we consult Phillips' rendering and find words that are more familiar, as follows:

1. it is from the Head . . .
2. that the whole Body as a harmonious structure
3. knit together by the joints with which it is provided
4. grows by the proper functioning of individual parts
5. to its full maturity in love

This makes things much clearer. Notice such words as *structure, knit together, joints, functioning,* and *maturity.* These are going to help us as we proceed further.

The central truth of the passage, we have decided, is "How the Church grows." Each section, 1 through 5, shows one cause or reason for this growth. Let us try to express each of these in a concise way without diverging from the text. Looking closely at our lists from both the King James Version and Phillips, we come up with:

How the Church Grows

1. The Church grows because of its union with the Head.
   . . . the Head, even Christ from whom . . .
2. It grows because of the uniqueness of its structure.
   . . . the whole body is fitly joined together.
3. It grows because of the ministry of its joints.
   . . . compacted by that which every joint supplieth . . .
4. It grows by the full contribution of each part.
   . . . according to the effectual working of every part.
5. It grows by the law of a living organism.
   . . . the edifying of itself. . . .

This is not the completed sermon: it is the outline or skeleton of one. It has to be clothed with flesh and develop muscle; but it has strong headings, adhering closely to the text. It is a unity—as is the Body—with its Head, skeleton, joints, parts, and principle of life.

Let us take another rather involved passage—Paul's speech on Mars' Hill, recorded in Acts 17:22-31. Read this through before proceeding further.

Paul knew that the many gods of the Athenians were proof of an innate desire to worship something, or someone, outside themselves. In his approach to these philosophers, he intended to make use of this fact: "I perceive . . . you are very religious" (RSV). Then he recalled seeing the altar to the UNKNOWN GOD courteously erected by the Athenians in case, in the multitude of their shrines, they had overlooked one deity.

To Paul, the omitted deity was the True and Living

God. So, he made his approach in this way. It was clever strategy. *"Whom therefore ye ignorantly worship, him declare I unto you."*

The Athenians' attitude is not too far removed from the thinking of many today. "I know I believe in God and that is as far as it goes," says a university student. Another says, "The thing to do is to be an agnostic. That way you always leave a way out if it turns out there is a God."

The unknown God is the way out—just in case. . . .

In our thinking, the central theme of the passage is THE UNKNOWN GOD. Looking carefully again we can see that Paul in his message had a plan—first, to bring this unknown god nearer and then into full focus. It will be helpful to set out each segment as before and then analyze each. To save space we will abbreviate:

1. God that made the world . . . He giveth to all life and breath and all things: verses 24, 25,
2. Hath made of one blood . . . and the bounds of their habitation: verse 26,
3. That they should seek the Lord . . . we ought not to think the Godhead is like unto gold . . . verses 27-29,
4. God . . . commandeth all men . . . to repent: verse 30,
5. He hath appointed a day . . . by that man: verse 31,
6. Him declare I unto you: verse 23.

Can you begin to see the structure of Paul's speech? and our message? Each segment tells us something about the unknown God and brings him nearer to us.

Now let us look at each segment more closely and see how it relates to the central theme—the unknown God. This may be expressed as follows:

1. The creatorship of God
2. The sovereignty of God
3. The proximity of God (His imminence)
4. The patience of God
5. The judgment of God
6. The experience of God

This is good: we have condensed into a few words the gist of each segment. But for preaching, we need something more gentle, less theological-sounding maybe because each of these points is going to be a heading in our sermon structure. They must be accurate, yet interest-sustaining. We want to be able to pass smoothly from one division to another. So, we improve our structure like this:

THE UNKNOWN GOD

1. He is the God of creation: verses 24, 25
2. He is the God of men, nations and history: verse 26
3. He is the God of human aspiration: verse 27
4. He is the God of revelation: verse 30
5. He is the God of the final examination: verse 31
6. He is the God who can be experienced: verses 23, 31

Paul brought his listeners step by step from the outmost fringes of creation, so to speak, to their own front door. He held them there by bearing down on their inborn sense of personal accountability to God; he knew that all men have this. Then he clinched the matter by his undeniable personal experience of this same God.

The Suggestive Method

Sometimes as we are reading the Bible a certain subject explodes in our mind, dropping stars like a firework rocket. Rereading the passage with this key thought in mind, we are often rewarded with a suggestive array of thoughts.

For example, reading on one occasion in Matthew 21, we came to a stop sign: "And Jesus went into the temple of God" (verse 12). This *suggested* the coming of Jesus into the believer's body (1 Corinthians 3:16). Is there an analogy between the two? Does the Bible tell us what Jesus did when He went into the Temple in Jerusalem? Does this illustrate what He does on entering His present-day temple—the body and being of a Christian?

With these questions bubbling, we turned with some excitement and read the passage again, noting the following:

1. He cast out all them that sold and bought *in the temple*: verse 12
2. He said, "*My house* shall be called a house of prayer": verse 13
3. The blind and the lame came to Him *in the temple*; and He healed them: verse 14
4. The children . . . *in the temple* . . . saying, Hosanna: verse 15
5. As He was teaching: verse 23 (i.e., in the temple)

How clear and purposeful was Christ's activity in that temple of stone and how beautifully it illustrates His potential ministry in these temples of flesh. Here is an edifying outline to follow.

CHRIST IN THE TEMPLE

1. He cleansed the temple: verse 12
2. He claimed the temple: verse 13
3. He healed in the temple: verse 14
4. He accepted worship in the temple: verse 15
5. He taught in the temple: verse 23

Take another illustration of the suggestive method. Musing in the great *resurrection* chapter, 1 Corinthians 15, we were held by the phrase, "*according to the scriptures*," in verses 3 and 4. Obviously, it is the Old Testament Scriptures that are referred to. The question arose: Which Old Testament Scriptures? "He rose again the third day according to the scriptures." What Old Testament Scriptures foretell the resurrection of Christ? This led to a search of the Old Testament for clues to the resurrection of Christ. We found the following which were like road signs to the motorist.

1. Noah's ark was God's survival plan for that day. It offered salvation for any who would heed and obey. When the Flood came, you were either in the ark and saved, or outside and lost—drowned in the waters of

judgment. The ark, therefore, is a picture of Christ bearing God's judgment upon the world at His death. When the waters assuaged, the ark came to rest on a renewed earth—so, Christ was raised, the work of salvation having been completed. Further details as to the very day on which the ark came to rest (Genesis 8:4, 5) are remarkable when compared with the day of Christ's resurrection; but we are not concerned with them here. Noah and his family began a new life in a new world.

2. The deliverance of Isaac on Mount Moriah is a picture of the resurrection of Christ from the dead (Genesis 22:5 and Hebrews 11:19).

3. The ceremony for the cleansing of a leper (Leviticus 14) required one sacrificial bird to be killed in an earthern vessel over running water—emblem of Christ dying. The second bird, with blood from the first on its wings, was turned loose and flew away—picture of Christ rising from the dead and taking tokens of his death into God's presence for acceptance.

4. The waving of the sheaf of firstfruits before the Lord at the time of reaping (Leviticus 23:9-12), is a picture of Christ's resurrection. It is so used by Paul in 1 Corinthians 15:20, 23.

5. The high rock which gave forth water for Israel is a picture of the Resurrection. God told Moses to speak to it; but Moses struck it, as previously he had smitten the low boulder in Horeb. For this error he was punished by God. In Horeb, the low rock was to be struck because it symbolized Christ being smitten on Calvary. The higher rock, representing Christ in resurrection power, was simply to be spoken to. The risen Christ will give the Holy Spirit "to them that *ask* Him."

6. Aaron's rod that budded, blossomed, and yielded almonds (Numbers 17) was God's confirmation of Aaron's priesthood. So, "Christ glorified not Himself to be made

an high priest; but he that said unto him, Thou art my Son, to day have I begotten thee" (Hebrews 5:5).

7. Jonah was used by Christ Himself as an illustration of His resurrection.

With these seven pictures of Christ's rising again, according to the Scriptures, we have seven prominent fundamentals confirmed:

1. Our new life in Christ—Noah
2. Redemption by substitution—Isaac's ram
3. Cleansing through the blood—leper
4. Life in eternity guaranteed—firstfruits
5. Outpouring of Holy Spirit—water from rock
6. High priesthood of Jesus—greater than Aaron
7. Final triumph over death—Jonah

Doubtless, there is too much material here for one sermon unless it is handled dexterously. A series of seven teaching messages would certainly be in place.

The Interrogative Method

This means setting out to answer, by means of the Scriptures, a question asked by a text. The answer is often close at hand; then sometimes we must "ride the range" of the Bible.

Take the following: "The Master saith, Where is the guest chamber, where I shall eat the passover with my disciples?" (Mark 14:14). Jesus was seeking a place where He could meet His disciples privately in fellowship and say special things to His men. Is He not hoping for a special place in your life where He may meet you—alone? Does He not say, "If any man hear my voice, and open the door, I will come in to him and sup with him"? (Revelation 3:20). The question is: Where is the guest chamber?

Christ gave His disciples detailed instructions and virtually answered the question: "He will show you a large upper room furnished and prepared: there make ready for us" (Mark 14:15). He, Jesus, describes what kind of place He wants. Let us set it out like this: the guest chamber must be

1. A *room*
2. An *upper* room
3. A *large* upper room
4. A large upper room *furnished*
5. A large upper room furnished and *prepared*

If Jesus is looking for the equivalent of this in your life, then the five details mentioned lend themselves to the development of a very personal message. The structure will certainly have unity, coherence, and proportion.

The Book of Job is, understandably, full of questions. Dr. G. Campbell Morgan preached a series on "Jesus' Answers to Job." This sounds like a fruitful field for study.

Here is another example: "While the Pharisees were gathered together, Jesus asked them, saying, What think ye of Christ?" (Matthew 22:41, 42). The context shows it had been a day of questions for Christ—loaded questions.

The Herodians—a political party—had tried to trap Him on the question of taxes (verses 16, 17).

Sadducces—the rationalists—had concocted a question about resurrection, an event in which they disbelieved (verse 28).

Pharisees—institutional religionists—hearing of the discomfiture of the other groups, had tried to put on the pressure by raising a question about the great commandment in the law (verse 36).

Christ's answers had amazed the politicians (verse 22), astounded the rationalists (verse 33), and silenced the traditionalists (verse 46).

Now it is Christ's turn to do the asking. His question is *the* question because it relates to the decisive factor of life—our attitude to the person of Christ, "What think ye of Christ?" All other matters—politics, philosophy, tradition —are puerile when compared with the answer to this one question: What think ye of Christ? He is the Eternal Hinge.

The answer could be built and the teaching applied by using the following structure:

1. What did people think of Christ then?
2. What do people think of Him now?
3. What do *you* think of Christ?

As suggestive answers to the question in section 1, above, we might have the following:

a. Some said He was mad: Mark 3:21, Phillips
b. Others said He was demon possessed: John 10:20
c. Many said He was a resurrected prophet: Matthew 16:14
d. Others were convinced He was the Son of God: Matthew 14:33; John 6:69.

This means—in that day—the answer to the great question showed:

a. Some ignored Him as being mad
b. Some opposed Him as devil-ridden
c. Some respected Him as a fine man
d. Some worshiped Him as divine and followed and served Him as Lord and Master

This structure offers great possibilities for development. Why not go ahead?

11
METHOD

Part II

In our discussion of types of sermon presentation, we now come to the fourth method.

The Connective Method

Sometimes we can link several texts that have a common relationship. In doing this, however, we must be careful that verses are not wrenched out of context just to give us what we want.

The Epistle to the Philippians is surely a favorite with most Christians. Rich views of truth lie between the "grace be unto you" at its beginning and the "grace be with you all" at its end. You cannot read this letter more than a few times—and remember it was written from jail—without sensing the vital importance of fellowship. The word, or its cognate, appears in every chapter. Notice:

1. Fellowship in the gospel: 1:5
2. Fellowship of the Spirit: 2:1
3. Fellowship of His sufferings: 3:10
4. Fellowship with my affliction: 4:14 (RV)
5. Fellowship in the matter of giving: 4:15 (RV)

Other versions use words such as *partnership, par-*

ticipation, sharing, working together, etc. Thus, we see that fellowship is more than just a warm feeling—it is the warp and woof of the Christian life.

Looking more closely into the five references above, we can see fellowship implies and is evidenced by:

1. United endeavor in gospel service: 1:5
   (*in furtherance of the gospel;* RV)
2. Mutual participation in the divine Spirit: 2:1
3. Acceptance of the sufferings of Christ: 3:10
4. Sharing of the sufferings of others: 4:14
5. Ready cooperation in provision: 4:15

Here is the start of a strong framework for future use. As a heart-moving conclusion to such a message, we suggest Moffatt's tender rendering of chapter 2, verses 1-4: "So by all the stimulus of Christ, by every incentive of love, by all your participation in the Spirit, by all your affectionate tenderness, I pray you to give me the utter joy of knowing you are living in harmony, with the same feelings of love, with one heart and soul, never acting for private ends or from vanity, but humbly considering each other the better man, and each with an eye to the interests of others as well as to his own." *Fellowship.*

In using the connective method, the link does not have to be, necessarily, a word—it may be an idea. Hebrews, chapter 10, draws a distinction between the bodies of animals offered in sacrifice and the body of Christ (see verses 1-6). The offering of the body of Christ was "once for all" (verses 10). His sacrifice opened the way for believers to enter the very presence of God (verse 20). Therefore, *the body of Jesus* is an important idea for our consideration. It was prepared for Him by God, "A body hast thou prepared me" (verse 5). When, in the inscrutable counsels of the Eternal, it was decided that God would visit and redeem the people of this planet, He decided to become one of them. This is indicated in verse 5; "Wherefore when he cometh into the world, he saith . . . a body hast thou prepared me."

Thinking over the significance of His body, in the earthly life of Jesus, we recall its prominence on the following occasions:

The birth: Luke 1:35; Hebrews 2:14, 16
The temptation: John 4:6, 7; Matthew 4:1-11;
            Hebrews 2:18
The transfiguration: Matthew 17:2
The crucifixion: John 19:7; 1 Peter 2:24; Hebrews 10:10
The resurrection: Acts 2:31, 32; cf. Luke 24:36-40
The ascension: Acts 1:9
The return: Acts 1:10, 11; cf. Zechariah 14:4 and 12:10.

These references help us to appreciate more fully the need and purpose of the divinely prepared body of Christ. From this, we might build a structure.

CHRIST'S DIVINELY PREPARED BODY

A body in which God became manifest to the world
A body in which He could experience temptation
A body that could be transfigured by divine glory
A body that could be crucified and die
A body that could be raised up from the dead
A body that could be glorified
A body in which He could visibly return and be recognized

This is a unified structure: it is coherent and proportionate. It stands solid on a scriptural foundation and exalts the Person and work of Christ. It brings before Christian people, in the judgment of this writer, truths they ought to know and—in fact—want to know.

For those who are interested, this sermon was condensed and written as an Easter meditation. It is reproduced here by permission of *The Pentecostal Evangel,* Springfield, Missouri.

CHRIST'S BODY

So far as we know, among the galaxies of planetary systems of which ours is but a small part, this small sphere on which we live is the only one to have been personally visited by Jesus, the Son of God. At some time, in the inscrutable counsels of the Eternal, it was decided and written in the volume of the Book that God would visit and redeem the people of earth whom He had created.

In order to accomplish this He would become one of them. He therefore prepared a body in which He could become manifest to the world: "Wherefore, when He cometh into the world, he saith ... a body hast thou prepared me" (Hebrews 10:5).

The birth of Christ was unique. His human body was directly begotten of the Holy Spirit. Mary, before she and Joseph came together, was "found with child of the Holy Ghost" (Matthew 1:18). Later a physician, investigating this phenomenon, recorded the words of the angel to Mary: "The Holy Ghost shall come upon thee, and the power of the Highest shall overshadow thee: therefore, also that holy thing which shall be born of thee shall be called the Son of God" (Luke 1:35). The body of Christ was divinely prepared in the womb of Mary.

C. H. Spurgeon expressed the wonder of the Incarnation: "Behold, O heavens, and thou earth, and ye places under the earth. Here is something worthy of your intensest gaze. Sit ye down and watch with earnestness, for the invisible God comes in the likeness of sinful flesh, and as an infant the Infinite hangs at a virgin's breast. Immanuel did not send, but *came*; He came in His own personality; in all that constituted His essential self He came forth from the ivory palaces to the abodes of misery; He came promptly at the destined hour; He came with sacred alacrity as one freely offering Himself." So exult all devout souls.

When Eve was made, God brought a motherless woman from the body of a man. When Jesus was born, God brought a fatherless man from the body of a woman.

Jesus, who was made man, was made in the likeness of man. He who created angels was made a little lower than the angels. A body was divinely prepared for the Incarnation.

In and through this prepared body Jesus experienced every kind of temptation and trial. By Jacob's well, for example, in noonday heat the Divine Visitor experienced human weariness and thirst (John 4:6, 7). In the lonely wilderness after long abstinence from food He was urged by Satan to satisfy miraculously His hunger pangs and, just this once, give the body priority over the spirit (Matthew 4:3, 4). Again, He was dared to play fast and loose with His body by leaping from the heights of a sacred building (verses 5, 7). He was, moreover, tempted to prostitute the use of that prepared body, just once, and so gain all the kingdoms of the world, by doing homage to Satan (verses 8, 10).

In Eden it was through the human body that sin entered, took up its abode, and showed its power; but, blessed be God, Christ, in His body, resisted and over-came temptation and sin and so counteracted the dire consequences to humanity.

"A body hast thou prepared me." For the accomplish-ment of redemption the Son of God needed a body in which (speaking with all reverence) He could be crucified and die. His body bore the overpowering weight of the cross, and He walked to "the place of a skull." It bore the crown of thorns and was made unsightly by the rivulets of blood so caused. The ungodly spat in His face, bruised His flesh by buffeting and scourging, and pierced His members with nails hammered home. They lacerated His body with a spear. Thus, all the world was shown what Satan, acting through unregenerate man, would like to do with the divine Victor.

Yet it was "in his own body on the tree" that He bore away our sins (1 Peter 2:24). It is "through the offering of the body of Jesus Christ" that all who believe can be saved and sanctified (Hebrews 10:10). The divinely prepared body is the redeeming body.

He dismissed His spirit at the victorious conclusion of the conflict, and His body expired, but His flesh did not decay as we would expect. It did not see corruption (Acts 2:31). It was soon raised up by God, for this was part of His mighty plan in the overthrow of the archfiend and ruler of the darkness of this world. Christ needed a body so that He might show Himself alive after His passion, and He did this to chosen witnesses when He said: "Behold my hands and my feet, that it is I myself: handle me, and see; for a spirit hath not flesh and bones, as ye see me have" (Luke 24:39, 40).

In furtherance of the divine purpose, Christ needed a body in which He could be taken up to heaven and glorified (Acts 1:9). This is known as "the body of His glory" (Philippians 3:21). At Bethany, on the eastern slopes of Olivet, while His hands were raised in benediction and blessing, "he was parted from them and carried up into heaven" (Luke 24:50, 51). Without His body, the watching disciples could not have been witnesses of His ascension.

And because of that body, when He returns, He will be recognized (Acts 1:11). His visible, bodily ascension requires His visible, bodily return. "His feet shall stand in that day upon the mount of Olives, which is before Jerusalem on the east" as predicted by the prophet even before the birth of Christ (Zechariah 14:4). Then, "they shall look upon me whom they have pierced, and they shall mourn for him, as one mourneth for his only son" (Zechariah 12:10). He needs and has a prepared body in which to return to this earth, not as visitor but as owner.

Until that day, He occupies and uses a spiritual body, of which the redeemed are members in particular (1 Corinthians 12:27). They are many members yet but one body (1 Corinthians 12:20). Through this spiritual body God intends to manifest Himself today, as He manifested Himself through the body of Jesus. The Church, His bride, is subject to much temptation, testing, and crucifixion as He was—always spiritually, sometimes physically so. Resurrection, ascension, and glorification are likewise the divine purpose for the spiritual body (Ephesians 2:4-7).

Then, "one day, Christ, the secret center of our lives, will show Himself openly, and you will all share in that magnificent dénouement" (Colossians 3:4, Phillips). "We don't know what we shall become in the future. We only know that, if reality were to break through, we should really reflect His likeness, for we should see Him as He really is!" (1 John 3:2, Phillips).

The Deductive Method

Bible language is rich in figures of speech. The truth is *literal;* the words employed may be *figurative.* "Literal language," says A. T. Pierson, "is often too narrow and cramped to afford ideas proper room and range, and hence a resort to figures of speech in which thought expands and enlarges the mind. Figures, instead of meaning less, mean more than literal terms, and are meant as an aid to fuller conception."

"A figure of speech," explains E. W. Bullinger, "is a designed and legitimate departure from the laws of language, in order to emphasize what is said. Hence, in such figures we have the Holy Spirit's overmarking, so to speak, of His own words."

There are several hundred figures used in the Bible. Here are a few of the better known:

Comparison, where one thing is compared to another: e.g., Psalm 84:10

Contrast, where two things are purposely set in opposition: e.g., Proverbs 11:1

Simile, likening one thing to another, in express terms: e.g., Psalm 103:11; Matthew 7:24-27

Metaphor, when one thing is used for another without expressing the likeness formally: e.g., Ephesians 2:19, 20

Parable, a narrative in which such likeness is drawn out: e.g., Isaiah 5; Matthew 13; Luke 14:16-24

Allegory, similar to a parable, only not, perhaps, capable of literal interpretation: e.g., Judges 9:7-15; Psalm 80:8-16

Type, where one thing supplies a suggestion or forecast of another. The Old Testament is full of these "ensamples" (1 Corinthians 10:11). They were written for our learning. "The typology of the Old Testament is the very alphabet of the language in which the doctrine of the New Testament is written" (Robert Anderson).

Apostrophe, where an individual or an attribute is addressed: e.g., Isaiah 51:9; 54:1-5; 1 Corinthians 15:55

Metonymy, representing a thing by one of its attributes or accompaniments: e.g., Galatians 6:17; Isaiah 59:1.

Figures of speech prompt homiletical thought. "They shall mount up with wings *as eagles*" (Isaiah 40:31), for instance, will bring us to think of the capacities and capabilities of this regal bird and so aspire to the lofty and triumphant life possible to those who "wait upon the Lord." After carefully pondering the figure used, we make certain deductions. These become the sermon structure. Here is an example.

In 1 Chronicles 29:15, King David, in one of his moments of great insight, confessed: "Our days on the earth are as a shadow, and there is none abiding." Others described his life rather differently and eulogized: "He died in a good old age, full of days, riches, and honor" (verse 28). David himself as his earthly course drew to a close apprehended reality: life is like a shadow.

So, we throw this idea around in our minds for a while. Maybe as we sit in our study we can see the ever-changing shadows cast by trees or buildings, and we begin to feel the aptness of the figure. A shadow is intangible; you cannot touch it as you can the object that casts it. As the earth moves round the sun, the shadow alters in angle and intensity: it rises to its zenith and then slowly declines. A shadow, therefore, is an imperfect outline. You continue ruminating, jotting down your thoughts as they come to you.

Your deductions can then be condensed and set in order; something like this, perhaps:

> The shadow is not the substance
> The shadow proves the reality of the substance
> The shadow is expressive of changefulness
> The shadow is but an imperfect outline

Upon a structure like this you can build your sermon. It may challenge those anticipating full satisfaction in this life, and it will appeal to them to consider the life which is eternal.

Suppose one morning we are reading the delightful 84th Psalm. We pause at verse 5: "Blessed is the man whose strength is in thee"; this we understand and know to be true. But we are not clear about the second phrase, "in whose heart are the ways of them." Seeking help, we turn to the Revised Standard Version and are encouraged to find this rendering: "in whose heart are the highways to Zion."

We proceed: "Who passing through the valley of Baca [weeping] make it a well [a place of springs, RSV]." This suggests a transformation that is truly delightful. With quickened desire we read on.

"They go from strength to strength." The people in this picture evidently are not weakened by their experiences in the painful valley; rather, it seems to increase their resources. "Every one of them in Zion appeareth before God": they all finish the journey and arrive in good shape.

We check these surmises with a reliable commentary and find we are indeed, looking in on a pilgrimage to the Temple at Jerusalem.

> Families journeyed together, making bands which grew at each halting place; they camped in sunny glades, sang in unison along the roads, toiled together over the hill and through the slough, and, as they went along, stored up happy memories which would never be forgotten" (*Treasury of David* by C. H. Spurgeon).

This is an apt picture of the life of a Christian with its varied experiences as he presses on toward heaven. How illustrative of the way God's grace can transform our painful, sorrowful experiences (Baca) into times of refreshing and progress. On their way to Jerusalem, the pilgrims cross dry sandy tracts and desolate places; but they dig pools or cisterns and so catch the early rains. The valley becomes a place of wells.

With this mental picture clearly before us, we now make our deductions or formulate the lessons we learn from the valley experiences.

> This experience is found only in the valley: *Baca*
> This experience gives character to the present life: *passing through . . .*
> This experience shows us God's all-sufficient grace: *make it a well . . . strength to strength*
> This experience makes us a blessing to others: *reservoirs for other pilgrims*
> This experience inspires us as to the final outcome: *every one . . . in Zion.*

Almost certainly there will be discouraged people in your congregation who will appreciate the insight and inspiration of a message like this.

The Categorizing Method

A preacher may at times feel the need to give plain, straightforward reasons for his belief of a doctrine or fact. He can do this by categorizing. An added advantage of this method is that it helps his listeners to crystalize their own beliefs.

Our Lord in the discourse in the upper room counseled His disciples, "Let not your heart be troubled" (John 14:1). Twice He uttered these words (see verse 27). His disciples, in other words, were to study to keep calm: they were not to allow their hearts to be burdened with anxiety. This was not just *chin up* talk by the Master. He knew there were good grounds for their serenity, a foundation for their peacefulness. As a matter of fact, these solid reasons are in our passage, so let us spotlight them. This will give us our sermon structure and at the same time lay a firm basis for confidence in the minds of our hearers.

REASONS WHY CHRISTIANS CAN BE PEACEFUL
John 14:1-27

1. We believe in God: verse 1
2. We believe Christ is coming again: verse 3
3. We have come to God through Christ: verse 6
4. We have a wonderful Father: verse 7
5. We have the privilege of prayer: verses 12-14
6. We have the indwelling of God: verses 16, 23
7. We have Christ's gift and promise of peace: verse 27

Here is another example. In 1 Corinthians, chapter 1, Paul mentions one of the problems troubling that church—sectarianism (verses 11 and 12). This leads him to make certain personal assertions why he feels his chief business is not to become involved in a personality cult but to preach the gospel. "Christ sent me not to baptize," he says, "but to preach the gospel" (verse 17). This was the preaching or message of the Cross.

Perhaps one day you will feel moved to declare why you consider this to be *your* chief concern in life. Even if you never preach such a message it would do you good to write down reasons why you are a preacher, or why you believe in preaching the gospel, or why you think preaching is the most worthwhile work. The categorizing of your thoughts will certainly be beneficial.

Coming back to Paul's personal affirmation, we might decide to list our reasons for preaching the gospel. Each one should be based on the Scripture and be explained in its setting. Here is a possible structure.

WHY I PREACH THE CROSS OF CHRIST

1. It is the chief theme of the Bible.
2. It was the great accomplishment of Christ's ministry.
3. It is the most uncompromising revealer of sin.
4. It is the only ground on which sin can be forgiven.
5. It is the supreme manifestation of God's love.
6. It is the sure pledge of final victory over evil.
7. It is a never-failing source of comfort to those who are saved.

This method lends itself to the presentation of doctrine. Under the title, "Why I believe in . . ." a personal declaration of faith can be made.

To repeat, this is one method of presentation. Obviously, you would not want to use it every Sunday. Our survey of methods is now concluded. There are other possibilities, but the beginner has sufficient for thought and practice.

Muscle

The days of preparation never end. Great and exacting discipline must be stringently exercised to keep from professionalism, laziness, pride, carelessness, distracting mannerisms and weaknesses. The church of Jesus Christ rises or falls according to the ideals and application of those who are set apart for the office of prophet. The daily devotional life, study habits and personal purity are necessary in the preparation of a sermon.

Physical discipline is an integral part of sermon preparation. Late rising, inadequate diet, and flabby muscles make for a sluggish mind. A secluded and private room, where distractions and interruptions will be at a minimum, will help make effective sermon preparation possible.

—J. Lester Harnish
We Prepare and Preach

12

MUSCLE

In the last few chapters we have been stressing the need for well-structured sermon outlines. Now we are going to think about putting flesh and muscle on these bones. A good idea, perhaps, will be to compose an imaginary sermon—step by step.

A sermon presupposes a text or a passage of Scripture as its basis. Sometimes the text just finds us: it clicks into place like the tumblers of a lock. We know without the shadow of a doubt what our message is to be, and we are as happy as a king.

More frequently, however, the word does not come to us unless we seek it. Perhaps we are thoughtfully looking through our stockpot (the file of texts and ideas we have been accumulating), and a text lights up for us like a road sign on a dark night. How thankful we are that we made a note of it and so kept it before us. Now we are beginning to enjoy the harvest of hard work, thought, and study.

We can be sure that in every congregation there are people who are

discouraged,
lonely,
have uncongenial jobs,
perplexed by domestic problems,
fighting an uneasy conscience.

You will know some of these because you have been visiting in their homes or talking with them. They probably are hoping for a word from the Lord. Their need will trigger your thoughts. Your private prayers for them and your objective attitude to their problems guides you in the Scriptures for an answer or an explanation. You can probably find a similar case history in your Bible.

There are signs that precede the birth of a baby, and there are recognizable evidences that a message is about to be born. It is not unlike the sensation an author has when he first glimpses the outline of a story. Edwin A. Peeples describes it like this:

> The first inkling an author should have that a story is about to occur is a sensation in the region of the heart. There should be a constriction, an ache, a quickening of excitement, an almost unbearable combination of delight and anguish. Upon this sensation, imagination and reason must work to shape an arrangement that will bring the same sensation to the reader.[*]

There it is—the pregnant, creative moment described by an artist.

By whatever means the text is settled upon, if it is to be used the next Sunday, the decision should be made as early in the week as possible. This will allow time for relaxed thinking and careful preparation. Andrew Blackwood is of the opinion that people remember a message for about as long as the preacher has thought about it before delivery. That is a challenging thought.

What does this text convey to *me?* Your answer to

---

[*]Edwin A. Peeples, A *Professional Storywriter'S Handbook* (New York: Doubleday & Co., Inc., 1960).

that single question is all-important. Does it say what I think it does? Consulting other versions at this point may help in answering this question. It must be remembered that the language of the Authorized Version, beautiful and beloved though it is, is seventeenth century English. It can be misunderstood. At a meeting for answering questions on the Bible, one problem submitted—in writing —was, "What are divers diseases?" The questioner was obviously confused by the suggestion of deep-sea activities in a Biblical incident. We can understand why.

We need to be quite decided, therefore, about what our text actually says, for it is our responsibility to handle God's Word honestly and reverently. What is important is not what we want a text to say, but what it does say. Our thinking, therefore, must focus on the heart of the text: its central truth. As we look through a magnifying glass held at some distance from the eyes, we can see several objects—enlarged, but blurred. To obtain the full advantage of the glass, you must make a proper adjustment—eye to lens to object. Then, sharpness of detail, texture, and shape of one object will stand out. You can preach "from Genesis to Revelation" out of one text if you choose; but it is far better for you—and your hearers— if you bring that one text into clear focus and detail.

Searching for the central truth is a vital matter. Time used on this is well spent. This search is closely related to the title of the sermon. The title you use for outside publicity may not be exactly the same as the one you affix to the sermon itself. In your outside or newspaper display, you are interested in catching the eye of the passerby, the casual attender, or the unchurched and so will choose words slanted to them. But the real title of a sermon is its central truth boiled down. This should be written out, revised, and pondered until it pertinently expresses the heart of the text. "No sermon is ready for preaching," said J. H. Jowett in his Yale Lectures, "nor ready for writing out, until we can express its theme in a short, pregnant sentence as clear as a crystal. I find the getting of that sentence is the hardest, the most exacting and the most fruitful labor in my study."

The sermon, then, must drive with all its power to one point. It must have a center of concentration, a point of focus. Like a target, this must be in front of you while you are composing the body of the sermon so that your work is unified and coherent.

If the choice of text is made early in the week, you will have time to brood on it, day and night, even when you are away from your study. Living with it like this establishes good rapport with it. Keeping it in your subconscious "incubator" will have surprising results. The Holy Spirit will brood upon it too. Remember, He did this at the creation and brought the cosmos out of chaos.

Sanctified imagination can liberate fresh thoughts and bring sparkling interest. Putting yourself in the story as, say, the central character or as an observer, will often open the door; thoughts will rush in like shoppers on sale day. Imagination is not to be confused with fantasy; it must always be bridled by reality.

Again, while it is necessary and legitimate to explain how Bible principles apply to this century, we must not try to interpret Palestinian customs by western culture.

The results of this far-ranging thinking should be brought together on a worksheet. It will be quite disordered at this stage and much of it may prove to be irrelevant, but you will have it before you.

John Albert Bengal produced a studious book called *The Gnomon of the New Testament*. A gnomon is the pin or column on a sundial that casts the shadow. Bengal's idea was that the force and meaning of the words and sentences in the New Testament are cast like a shadow on its pages by the text. His *Essay on the Right Way of Handling Divine Subjects* is quoted, in brief, by C. H. Spurgeon in *Commenting and Commentaries,* as follows:

> Put nothing *into* the Scriptures, but draw everything from them, and suffer nothing to remain hidden, that is really in them.
>
> Though each inspired writer has his own manner and style, one and the same Spirit breathes through all, one grand idea pervades all.
>
> Every divine communication carries (like the diamond) its own light with it, thus showing whence it comes; no touchstone is required to discriminate it.
>
> The true commentator will fasten his primary attention on the *letter* (literal meaning), but never forget that the Spirit must equally accompany him; at the same time we must never devise a more spiritual meaning for Scripture passages than the Holy Spirit intended.
>
> The *historical* matter of Scripture, both narrative and prophecy, constitute as it were the *bones* of its system, whereas the *spiritual* matters are as its muscles, blood vessels and nerves. As the *bones* are necessary to the human system, so Scripture must have its *historical* matters. The expositor who nullifies the *historical* groundwork of Scripture for the sake of finding only spiritual truth everywhere, brings death on all correct interpretations. Those expositions are the safest which keep closest to the text.

These are excellent guiding principles for the preacher.

Perhaps by this time you can see your text has natural divisions. They are so obvious that you write them down at once; they are the sermon's structure. Suppose, for instance, you were thinking of Philippians 4:19. "But my God shall supply all your need according to His riches in glory by Christ Jesus." You might see three divisions.

My God shall supply: *A Gracious Promise*
All your need: *A Full Provision*
According to His riches: *A Sure Guarantee.*

Everything discussed in this chapter so far can be considered as spade work. The soil has been roughly turned and is now ready for the rake. This will break it down further and give it a fine tilth.

Go to your lexicon and see what you can discover about the precise meaning of the leading words in your text.

Make a note of illustrations that have come to mind.

Do all this before you look at a commentary. Not that we are against them. "A respectable acquaintance with the opinions of the giants of the past," said Spurgeon, "might have saved many an erratic thinker from wild interpretations and outrageous inferences." What we advocate, however, is that as much original thought as possible be given to the text before commentaries are consulted; otherwise your sermons could become merely a rehash of the commentators. You want your listeners, if possible, to share what you have seen for yourself. The truth is to be mediated through *your* personality.

If you do not have the main divisions of your sermon, now is the time to work on them. Build a good structure. Let the divisions be natural—not far-fetched—helpful to thought and memory; strongly suggestive; distinct—not overlapping each other; logical, so as to carry your hearers with you; and connected, so as to maintain interest. Alliteration can help if it is not strained.

Your structure is your plan of campaign. It is a carefully constructed outline of your thinking. It will expand and guide your mind while you are preaching. Remember, a preacher who rambles when preaching has not disciplined himself in the study.

Clothing the structure comes next. Two or three subheadings will be necessary in each main division. These too should have the qualities of unity, coherence, and proportion.

It is at this stage that your central reference index is particularly useful. With regard to this, we quote a gardener, "The only way to garden successfully is to begin the year before last." Any filing system will not come into its own for a few years, until some treasures have been stored away in it.

The fruit of your reading, your clippings, and your recorded illustrations are now tapped and flowing into the material you have massed on your work sheet. It is a wonderful moment when you lay your hand on the perfect illustration for a point in your sermon.

Suppose you are working on the text, "Joseph is a fruitful bough, even a fruitful bough by a well; whose branches run over a wall" (Genesis 49:22). Four leading thoughts are in this verse:

Joseph is a bough: i.e., a living part of the tree
He is a fruitful bough: i.e., a fruitbearing branch
Even a bough by a well: i.e., he has deep resources
Whose branches run over the wall: i.e., his fruit-
     fulness is unusually extensive

The central truth relates to the prolific fruitfulness of Joseph, the cause and consequences of it. So, the four leading thoughts could be expressed like this:

His vital union: *a branch*
His healthy condition: *a fruitful branch*
His unique position: *by a well*
His remarkable expansion: *over the wall.*

Each of these points can be appropriately illustrated from the life story of Joseph and hardly need anything further. But suppose in developing the second section you wanted to explain that one reason for Joseph's fruitfulness was that God pruned him. The idea might send you to your filing system and under "Pruning" you would find the illustration given on page 78. Can you see how useful this would be in explaining God's ways with the Christian?

Much of the material you have gathered together on your work sheet will have to be eliminated. It may hurt you not to use some of this fine material; but remember, a sermon is not an exhibition of knowledge; it is the impartation of a divine principle. Cutting may be called a gentle art, but it is inevitably severe. Therefore, regard it as a sharpening of the arrowhead. Be objective, be critical. Brevity is better than blur. The danger of aimless wandering in preaching is that some of the hearers get lost.

A salesman studies his approach to a customer to gain a hearing. He may start with a question, a problem, or difficulty. The introduction to a sermon should be brief and relevant. Fifteen minutes is far too long to spend on vapid generalities or insipid truisms. Get to the message of the Word as soon as possible; don't dither in the doorway.

A time-honored introduction is to announce the text. If the minister holds God's Word and preaching in high esteem, so will his congregation. A reverential attitude rubs off on people. Surely we need not apologize for expecting people to bring their Bibles and refer to them. When we have announced our text, however, let us give folk time to get to the starting place.

After this, a few brief comments on the subject and its context are all that is needed before launching into the message. A printed sermon titled, "He Walked with God," told the story of Enoch. The introductory paragraph was as follows:

> To read the "book of the generations of Adam" in Genesis 5 is like peering into an old cemetery. With monotonous regularity we can almost hear the tolling of the bell. The theme of verses three to five is rung over and again: "Adam lived an hundred and thirty years, and begat a son in his own likeness, after his image; and called his name Seth: and the days of Adam after he had begotten Seth were eight hundred years: and he begat sons and daughters: and all the days that Adam lived were nine hundred and thirty years: and he died," Some lived longer, others begat more children, but one experience was common to them all—*they died* (verses 8, 11, 14, 17, 20,

27, 31). The sexton at the old cemetery was never without his job of tolling the bell.

Another time, a few well-chosen words that say "wake up" to the mind are appropriate. Here as an example is an introduction to a sermon based on Psalm 122:1

An invitation from the White House addressed to you personally, would cause more than a flutter of excitement. A man receiving a command to appear before his monarch, would consider himself highly honored. For the greater to invite the lesser is to bestow a favor. So, when King David was invited by some friends to go to the Temple to worship, he looked upon it as an honor from God: "I was glad when they said unto me, Let us go into the house of the Lord."

Briefly stating a problem—if the sermon is going to solve it—can arouse interest. A sermon structured on Jesus' words, "What I do thou knowest not now; but thou shalt know hereafter," commenced this way:

The atmosphere in the Upper Room was tense with drama. An hour or so before, twelve sullen men had stomped up the stairs to eat supper with Christ. There had been no servant to attend to the usual refreshing of each guest on his arrival, but the proprietor had thoughtfully placed in a corner a pitcher of water, a basin, and a towel.

Normally, without thinking twice about it, one of the men would have offered to bathe the tired feet of his companions. He would have done it as automatically as any man today would offer to assist a friend with coat and hat. But this occasion was different. The apostles had been arguing about their respective positions in the Kingdom—about who should be the greatest—and there were about twelve different opinions.

A well-told story will usually secure attention, but you need care and skill in making transition from the story to the sermon. Generally, stories are easier to handle in the course of the message or at its end.

Occasionally if the main headings of the sermon are exceptionally good, they can be given away as an introduction; their quality will hold the listeners' interest.

But usually it is better to keep each division until you come to it; you make use of the hearers' curiosity in this way.

When you come to "and lastly" let it be just that. An optimist, it has been said, is a lady who slips on her shoe when the preacher says, "and finally. . . ." You should know how you are going to bring your message to a close else you will be like a man driving round looking for a parking place.

For a sermon that has used reasoning or argument, *brief recapitulation* is a good idea.

Devotional and ethical sermons lend themselves to a *personal application.* This goes for the evangelistic message too.

The *how-to* explanation can suitably terminate a sermon stressing a Christian duty.

A apt *illustration* can often summarize and drive home the truth taught. Here is the conclusion to the sermon on Enoch:

> No one wanted Enoch around any more. He was a "square." He did not fit in with the boastful, arrogant, flattering crowd. It is a wonder they let him live so long. But he had been a friend of God for three hundred years. Maybe one day after walking and witnessing, God said to him, "Enoch, I can see no one wants you down here; why not walk over to my home just a little further on?" So, "He was not: for God took him." He was translated, transferred to an upper room of God's universe. He was caught up, just as thousands of living Christians (those who walk with God) will, at the coming of Christ, "be caught up . . . in the clouds, to meet the Lord in the air: and so shall we ever be with the Lord" (1 Thessalonians 4:17).
>
> "Just a closer walk with Thee . . . let it be, dear Lord, let it be."

In the last chapter we used 1 Chronicles 29:15 as an example for structuring. We now give the full outline so that the subdivisions, introductions and conclusion can be seen.

THE SHADOW OF LIFE

Text: Our days on the earth are as a shadow, and there is none abiding. 1 Chronicles 29:15.

Intro: The historian's comment on David's life was quite different: cf. verse 28: "He died in a good old age, full of days, riches, and honor." David's life had been long, full, rewarding.

But notice what he said of his own life: ". . . a shadow. . . ."

Closing words of great men are worthy of note.

I. The Shadow is not the Substance.
   A. The full life is yet to be.
      1. This transient life of about 70 years is a speck in the stream.
      2. Eternal Life (Life of the Ages) is the real.
   B. A shadow may instruct us; it cannot satisfy us.
      Foolish to be absorbed with the shadow and neglect the substance
   C. Satan deceives many into thinking this life is the sum total of reality,
      cf. RICH FOOL: Luke 12:16
      But see Psalm 17:13b-15: (NB, *satisfied*)
      David had plenty of this world's goods but knew the real thing was eternal life.

II. The Shadow proves the reality of the Substance.
   A. Where there is a shadow, a substance must have cast it. So, present life proves there is a life-to-be.
   B. Men know this intuitively:
      1. Because of moral accountability: Romans 2:5-9
         We know we must give some explanation of our lives to our Creator.
      2. Because of justice: Psalm 94:1-7
      3. Because of reward: Matthew 25:31, 32
   C. If adjustments are not made in this life, they must be in the fuller life to come.

III. A Shadow is expressive of Changefulness.
   A. Because the earth is continually moving, shadow alters.
      1. Rising sun—slight shadow: birth, early days
      2. Noon sun—strong shadow: life at its zenith
      3. Setting sun—weakening shadow: declining years
   B. We are beginning to die from moment of birth.

Life: sum total of forces that resist death
C. Words spoken can never be recalled.
D. Opportunities lost can never be regained.
Illus: Man at funeral of David Livingstone: I. 1/52
"Swift to its close ebbs out life's little day . . . ."

IV. A Shadow is but an imperfect Outline.
A. All the best things in this life will be found in perfection and fulness in the next.
1. "Now we see through a glass darkly but then face to face. . . ."
2. "Now we know in part . . ."
B. Here, life beset with cares, griefs
There, no more death, crying, sorrow, pain.
C. Here, life marred through partings
There, forever with the Lord.
D. Now, we serve proving the will of God.
Then, we shall serve Him perfectly.
E. All the worst things in life will be repeated in the final accounting.
1. Separation: Revelation 22:15
2. Fixity: Revelation 22:11

Conclusion: You can determine the character of your after life.
If you seek God, through Christ, there is mercy, forgiveness, eternal life.
If you ignore God, spurn the grace of Christ, you put yourself outside God's mercy.
Turn to Christ; come to Him; trust Him; rejoice.

Manifesto

"And his name is called the WORD OF GOD." Christ is God articulate. Our Lord is the word of absolute infallibility; the word of exhaustless depth; the word of irresistible power; the word of perfect pardon; the word of unlimited healing; the word of almighty succour; the word of inexhaustible love; the word of eternal holiness; the word of final judgment."

—D. M. Panton
The Godhead of Jesus

13

MANIFESTO

Webster defines *manifesto:* "A public declaration of motives and intentions by a government or by a person or group regarded as having some public importance." Our use of the word has this sense: a public declaration of God's saving purpose by a preacher, as being of the utmost possible importance. When you stand in the pulpit, you can be invested with the greatest authority and dignity that God ever gave to man.

You are in a courtroom. As a minister of reconciliation, you have authority to speak the word of pardon to the culprit and the rebel. You are to tell them of the One *who forgiveth all . . . iniquities.* Your manifesto is of pardon and freedom.

You stand among the sick and wounded. In your congregation are those who need heart surgery, mental renewal, spiritual adjustment; the bruised, the hurt, the weak are looking to you. Tell them of the One *who healeth all . . . diseases.* Your manifesto declares the possibility of the restoration and rehabilitation of the total man.

You stand in the marketplace where souls are being

auctioned. Your message is of liberty for the slave because a ransom has been paid. This redemption has not been transacted in the corruptible coinage of the world but by the sacrifice of the Son of God at Calvary. Your manifesto, therefore, joyfully announces One who *redeemeth* thy life from destruction. The pitiable slave may know the joy of becoming God's own, of having a deep personal sense of belonging.

You are to go further. To the forgiven, the healed, the redeemed you are to make known that their Benefactor is the One who *crowneth . . .* with *lovingkindness* and *tender mercies.* Salvation includes rescue from sin and perdition, but it is more than this: it is a shining pathway to coronation.

Your manifesto, therefore, offers an invitation to a royal banquet. The host? He who satisfieth thy mouth with good things. Surely our God is real and has done great things for us. *Bless the Lord, O my soul* (Psalm 103).

You are a *minister of God.* Remember, "We use no hocus-pocus, no clever tricks, no dishonest manipulation of the word of God. We speak the plain truth and so commend ourselves to every man's conscience in the sight of God" (2 Corinthians 4:2, Phillips).

You are a *preacher.* "It is Christ Jesus the Lord Whom we preach, not ourselves." (2 Corinthians 4:5, Phillips). The ways in which this self-hiding is brought about are costly but rewarding: "We are handicapped on all sides, but we are never frustrated; we are puzzled, but never in despair. We are persecuted, but we never have to stand it alone: we may be knocked down but we are never knocked out! Every day we experience something of the death of the Lord Jesus, so that we may also know the power of the life of Jesus in these bodies of ours" (2 Corinthians 4:8-10, Phillips). This is rough treatment, but it makes us preach Christ—not ourselves. It is the only way our aptitude for self-glorification can be checked. Self-recognition, self-approval and self-vindication so often get in the way of Christ Jesus the Lord. Every emotion within us has its own silent voice and, somehow, gets through beyond the words we use.

You are a *witness*. There are many kinds of evidence; some of the principal types are as follows:

1. Evidence derived from *testimony*. You can hear Peter using this when preaching in the house of Cornelius, "To Him give all the prophets witness . . ." (Acts 10:43).

2. Evidence of *authority*. In the courts the opinions of learned men upon particular subjects are produced and allowed. So, in the Scripture we have a complete system or body of evidence. Quoted correctly and interpreted fairly, we may say, "Thus saith the Lord."

3. Evidence of *experience*. Paul uses this in Romans 7:5-25. Summing up in verse 21, he says: "I find then a law, that, when I would do good, evil is present with me." The argument continues in chapter 8, where the inward witness of the Spirit is called upon (verse 16).

4. Evidence from *comparison and contrast*. "Are there any among the vanities of the Gentiles that can cause rain? or can the heavens give showers? art not thou he, O Lord our God? therefore we will wait upon thee: for thou hast made all these things" (Jeremiah 14:22).

5. Evidence of *probability*. Again, listen to Paul in his defense before Agrippa: "Why should it be thought a thing incredible with you, that God should raise the dead?" (Acts 26:8).

6. Evidence of the *senses*. How forcefully John uses this in his first Epistle: "That which was from the beginning, which we have heard, which we have seen with our eyes, which we have looked upon, and our hands have handled, of the Word of life . . . declare we unto you" (1 John 1:1, 3).

7. Evidence by *analogy* can be used as an auxiliary as it is, for instance, in Romans 6.

8. Evidence by *inference*. Notice: "He who hath builded the house hath more honor than the house. For every house is builded by some man; but he that built all things is God" (Hebrews 3:3, 4).

Preaching is a declaration, a declaration aimed at persuading the hearers, be they unbelievers or Christians. We preach for a verdict, a decision.

The decision maker at the center of our being is our will; this is the rudder that determines the course of our actions. "We are not in this world so much for the exercise of our intellects," said Wesley, "as for the exertion of our wills." He put the emphasis where it should be.

"Man never wills save under the impulse of a conviction." G. Campbell Morgan's statement carries us a step further. Modern advertising, for instance, is aimed at people's wills: it presses them to decide for a certain product. Millions of dollars are spent annually to convince you that you need a certain soap, toothpaste, or alcohol. The target, always, is your will. Everything possible is done to persuade you and make you decide to believe what is said or visualized.

"In this day of decision," writes G. C. Parker, "many of our churches are found wanting. Instead of presenting the Christian faith as demanding decision, they have offered it as a pleasant philosophy, a nice code of ethics, a kind of religious milltown. The Bible is a book of decisions. In both the Old Testament and the New Testament, it confronts men with the inescapable necessity of making up their minds. It unashamedly competes for men's minds."

Reducing this matter to simple proportions, then, we repeat—the target at which we must aim is the will of our hearers. Without dogmatizing, it seems that the term *heart*, used so frequently in the Bible, refers to the will—reigning as king but attended by two counselors—the feelings and the mind. This is the spring from which issue the streams that make up the individual life in its totality. The heart of the heart is the will.

The diagram shows the two approaches to the will.

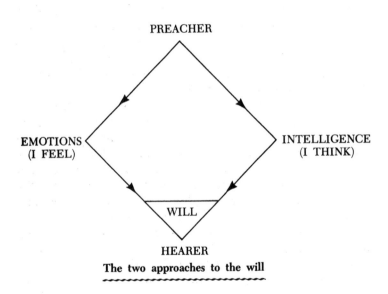

The two approaches to the will

The will, it can be seen, is approached through (1) the emotions, and (2) the intelligence. These are also the avenues through which Satan tempts us. He too aims to capture the citadel of the will and cause it to surrender. If the will remains firm, the temptation fails; if it yields, the temptation succeeds. The preacher's approach and objective is the same, except he wants to persuade the will to yield to God.

A message may stir the hearer's emotions—it often will, and there is nothing wrong with this. The gospel is a love story. The poignancy of the Cross can move the hardest to tears. But it must be remembered, the will—not the emotions—is the target. Preaching planned to arouse emotional feeling and nothing else is emotionalism. It is rightly condemned. Unless preaching has in view a thrust upon the will, it is failing of its purpose. It has been said that when a resolve or a fine feeling is allowed to evaporate without bearing practical fruit (in decision and action) it is worse than a chance lost.

Another message will offer information and reasoning and so approach by way of the intelligience. Here again, if its purpose is simply to satisfy intellectual or philosophical questions, it is little more than intellectualism. At the risk of being wearisome, we repeat: it is the will that must be challenged. Most people respond more readily to one of these two approaches; the preacher, therefore, is advised to vary his line—but not his target.

Again, some hearers think that unless there is emotional arousal that can be "felt" a message is without value. Others always want intellectual fulfillment—as if they were emotionless beings. Both are wrong. Balanced ministry will meet both types of need. The emotion-conscious need a message to stimulate their thinking, and intellectuals need infusions of Bible-inspired enthusiasm.

When the will makes its decision because the person both knows and feels this is right, there is the most desirable situation. No doubt Fenelon had good reasons for saying that true religion resides in the will alone.

The prerogative of man's will is frightening, but it is not absolute. Tennyson had a unique way of explaining it:

Our wills are ours, we know not how;
Our wills are ours to make them Thine.

A preacher had a brother who was a baseball player. "Why is it," he asked wistfully, "that for delivering a ball across a plate you get ten times as much as I do for delivering a sermon?"

The reply came promptly, "I guess it's all in the delivery, brother." The man had a point.

Some sermons in their delivery remind one of a bludgeon. Whack follows whack in an unending torrent of words. Power seems to be measured by breathlessness, hoarseness, and perspiration. The display reminds one of the time when "a great and strong wind rent the mountains, and break in pieces the rocks before the Lord; but. . . ."

"We are not the passive communicators of infallibility," said Spurgeon, "but the honest teachers of such things as we have learned so far as we have been enabled to grasp them." Humility goes well with authority in the pulpit.

Then there is the dominating preacher who would override everyone by the force of his personality. A certain type of hearer responds to this—even depends on it and will go miles to get it. But self-adulation and pomposity don't need exhibition; they need crucifixion.

At the other extreme is the casual delivery, aimless and pointless. This preacher says, "take it or leave it." Most leave it.

The preaching of Jesus had two notable qualities. "All bare him witness and wondered at the gracious words which proceeded out of his mouth" (Luke 4:22). *Gracious words.* "He taught them as one having authority" (Matthew 7:29). *Authoritative words.* His preaching, like the Master Himself was "full of grace and truth." May the words and manner of our delivery be as close to the Master as that.

A modern communications expert writes: "The virtues of informational language are—precision (accuracy), clarity and brevity."*

Precision. Your words are your projection lens; your vocabulary is you. Your lens needs to be kept clean, polished, and adjusted if the word picture is to come through.

Writing is good for preachers; it makes them choosy about words. Bacon's dictum is worth recall: "Reading maketh a full man; speaking maketh a ready man and writing maketh an accurate man." Writing practice will help a preacher who wants to make sure he is understood. In America, probably greater care is needed than elsewhere because of the diversity of its peoples.

You can develop a taste for words. Your ear can be trained to appreciate the harmony of words as they can musical sounds. Habitual use of the dictionary and watching the way writers and speakers use them will cause you to fall in love with words. "Every word in our language," say Funk and Lewis, "is a frozen metaphor, a frozen picture." It is this poetry behind words that gives language its overwhelming power. So, without being fussy, try being selective about the words you use; then you will not be tempted to rely on the art of "making deep noises from the chest sound like important messages from the brain."

Words have changed the current of history. They have undoubtedly altered the direction of your life. They can also be a turning point for your hearers. And they will if you try to be as accurate as possible.

The preaching of trial sermons in college and seminary

---

*Bess Sondel, *Power Steering with Words* (Chicago: Follett Publishing Company, 1964).

is to be encouraged. There should be more of it. The criticism of fellow students may be hard to take, but it can save embarrassment later. A congregation that were treated to the following mixture at the conclusion of a sermon might have received the general idea of what it was "all about," even if, temporarily, they were puzzled. "The work begun today," exhorted the preacher, "may kindle a spark which will only need watering to make it a great fire that will spread and multiply till all the fowls of the air can sit on it."

Clarity. What is the use of the finest sermon if it cannot be heard or is heard only in parts? Distinctness of articulation is vital. While we do not wish in preaching to give the impression we are addressing the deaf, we do want to avoid mumbling, slurring, and monotony. According to an expert, we have at least 72 muscles to help us pronounce the words we use. So, why try to get by using 27? Twenty-seven million dead letters were handled by the Post Office Department in one year recently. Don't let your verbal letters get lost on their way to your hearers.

Brevity. Cutting down our words adds to their forcefulness and impact; it is also fine discipline for our thought processes. A time limit as, for instance, on a radio message, compels a speaker to make the most of his words—it makes him pack the punch. This is good for the pulpit preacher too; otherwise he may float around in a sea of words. While his own boat may survive, many others may submerge.

It is questionable whether people hear as much as we think they do. The University of Minnesota, after giving listening tests, concluded the average person is a half-listener. To remedy this, the University gave listening courses and claims that every group trained averaged better than a 25% gain in proficiency.

The above paragraph, of course, might be used as an argument for longer sermons; but another factor has to be considered—the span of attention given by the average listener. In these days of stacato newscasts, spot announcements, condensed books, and visual programs controlled by the flip of a switch, many people have lost their power of concentration; it has slowly ebbed away. So, it is doubtful whether Mr. Average Man will listen to a sermon that goes on for more than thirty minutes, unless he is in great need of soul. But thirty minutes is ample time for a preacher who has studied, prayed, and prepared a strong, well-illustrated outline. Without wasting time at the beginning of the message, he can come straight to the point and make every minute count. It is far better that people wish you had gone on longer than that you had stopped ten minutes earlier.

Some men, having written out their sermons in full, preach from the manuscript. This method has merit. It means that every word spoken has been thought out and chosen. It means also that the time required for delivery of the message is known. Its demerit is that it restricts spontaneity and, possibly, the momentary leading of the Holy Spirit.

Other men use no notes in the pulpit. Some memorize their message and then recite it. Others commit their structured outline to memory and regard this as sufficient. Some do not believe in any notes; they open their Bibles and start speaking, trusting their every word will be inspired. The method used must, obviously, be according to the nature and temperament of the preacher.

Probably the most practical method is to have your outline in front of you as you preach. If you have given much thought to the preparation of this, it really represents the essence of what you want to say. Its main headings and subdivisions have been built into position;

they are a condensation of your thinking. As you preach they will bring back the fuller thought to your mind. At the same time, because of their brevity, your eyes will not be tied to the notes but will be free to look into the faces of your hearers. There will be no barrier between preacher and people.

Moreover, an outline allows you to enjoy the inspiration of the moment and any special leading from God. Without an outline a preacher can easily jump about from thought to thought without connection or aim. He will confuse his listeners and weary them as he backtracks over an area of his subject already mentioned. Other advantages of an outline will be considered in the next chapter.

We come, now, to the preacher's supreme asset . . . the divine plus: the unction from the Holy One. This all-important gift, however, is not a substitute for diligent study and preparation. It is not intended to compensate for a man's weakness in his devotions or his ethical shallowness. But without it, all the rest will lack conviction and life.

Lecturing to ministerial students, C. H. Spurgeon said: "We have been raised from the dull sphere of mere mind and matter into the heavenly radiance of the spirit-world; and now, as spiritual men, we discern spiritual things, we feel the forces which are paramount in the spirit realm, and we know there is a Holy Ghost for we feel Him operating upon our spirits." Without a copious anointing of the Holy Spirit resting upon us, our office is a mere name; we cannot speak convincingly for Christ or perform His commission. It is the Spirit who takes of the things of Christ and reveals them; we are helpless without that gracious assistance. He gives light to accompany the truth and adds divine authority to our words. He gives freedom of utterance so that we feel a live coal has touched our lips. He restrains the unwise word, the out-of-place humor, the unbecoming reference. He is our energy to accomplish the impossible task, the lifter of our burden, and the joy of our souls.

He makes us blessedly aware of the Christ behind us as we declare the whole counsel of God. He makes us feel our subject until it thrills us and we are borne as on eagles' wings. He gives us compassion, yearning, and persuasive power. He searches the heart of the Christian and pricks the conscience of the unsaved that they might repent and turn to Christ. Lloyd George, speaking of the preaching of John Elias, a Welsh evangelist, said that when he described the Almighty letting fly the arrows from His bow, the whole congregation instinctively parted in two to allow passage for the shaft . . . so great was the conviction.

The anointing of the Holy Spirit upon a preacher is not a blessing automatically his when he enters a church or because he is a preacher. E. W. Sangster points out a threefold preparation is necessary. It will be noticed that this is the burden of this book.

1. The preparation of *the whole life*. Through the passing days, a minister has the opportunity of developing intimate communion with His God. It has been stated more than once in these pages that the whole of life is a preparation for preaching. It is our duty to "give ourselves to prayer and the ministry of the Word." It is the devil's business to keep us from doing so. If he can sidetrack us by distractions that look legitimately religious, he will do so. Unfortunately, he has tremendous success. It is easy to feel that slipshod devotions—for one day, or a "borrowed" sermon—for one time, make no difference. But we are wrong if we do so. "For the want of a nail the shoe was lost . . . the battle was lost." The jingle is well known. A man's pulpit ministry is closely related to what he is and does from Monday morning to Saturday night. His

vocation must become his life. This has been the burden of the first chapters of this book.

2. The preparation of *the day*. Honesty with each day's time and diligence in the study during the days preceding the Sunday are here referred to. We have called this *particular preparation*. All praise be to God that while studying we can know that unction from God. It is an unforgettable experience when the unfolding of the Word fills you with such delight that you feel transported to the threshold of heaven. The pen is laid down, the heart melts, the worship cascades, the soul is astonished; vocal cords are loosed, the spirit dances, and your room becomes none other than the house of God. With gladness we shout, "I rejoice at thy word, as one that findeth great spoil" (Psalm 119:162).

Gloating over our newly discovered spoil and storing it in our treasury we feel like the disciples may have done after listening to the Master's incomparable teaching in His parables of the Kingdom.

"Have ye understood all these things?" He asked. They said unto Him, "Yea, Lord."

Then He said, "Therefore every scribe which is instructed [in] the kingdom of heaven is like unto a man that is an householder, which bringeth forth out of his treasure things new and old" (Matthew 13:51, 52).

3. The preparation of *the moment*. It is a known fact that dedicated musical performers will not only practice for long hours, but they will demand to be left alone—in silence—for a period of self-preparation before an actual performance. Concentration in purpose, freedom from distracting thoughts, and a sense of unity with their art is what they seek. A minister, whose vocation is the highest of all, needs all this—and more.

When he enters the pulpit, he should be as one immediately from the presence of God. Prescribing time has its perils, yet, twenty minutes alone with God would seem to be a minimum before the commencement of a service. The utilitarian habit or working right up to the starting moment is, to say the least, inappropriate. A preacher is blessed, indeed, if he has a handful of members that come to church adequately prepared in heart and mind through waiting upon God. But let him not assume their personal preparation can replace his.

Nothing is more important than that the man of God be just that—the man of God—when he stands before the congregation. Minds will be tuned to many other wavelengths; and thoughts, like stage dancers, will waltz by for attention. How wise is a pastor who can educate his people to engage in silent prayer or Bible meditation before a service. Thoughts have to be corralled—brought into captivity, attention arrested, and spirits attuned to the voice of the Holy Spirit. The minister himself must have his own spirit deeply anchored; he must be divinely mantled and united with his God. Then a holy emanation from him will spread over the congregation "like the precious ointment upon [Aaron's] head ... that went down to the skirts of his garments; as the dew of Hermon, and as the dew that descended upon the mountains of Zion: for there the Lord commanded the blessing, even life for evermore" (Psalm 133:2, 3).

Then will the preaching be anointed and the eyes of the peoples' understanding enlightened. The disciples will be glad because they have seen the Lord.

Young man, apprentice preacher, heed these words. Do not take your example from those who cheapen preaching, who regard a service as a program or display to be put on, whose one concern is numbers and whose idea is to copy modern entertainment as closely as possible. They have their reward. Study, rather, the spirit of the men of the Bible: Elijah, persevering in prayer; Daniel, seeking purity rather than promotion; John the Baptist, fiery in his solitude; and Paul, glorying in his infirmities that the power of Christ might rest upon him. Bend heart and mind, soul and strength to the one commission that is yours, to "preach the word . . . watch . . . endure . . . and do the work of an evangelist, make full proof of thy ministry" (2 Timothy 4:2, 5).

In preaching, application is the art of fitting the truth to personal, contemporary needs. Its purpose is to make each individual in the congregation feel "thou art the man." The art calls for wisdom and tact because most of us while we are prepared to see the glove fit another's hand are slow to try it on our own. We are like a Scottish listener who, commenting on the morning sermon, said, "It was vera well if it hadna been for the trash of duties at the hinna end."

Some sermons lend themselves to a gentle, point by point application—as they proceed. With these, a little more pressure can be applied at the conclusion.

Recapitulation—but brief—can be used to good effect too; sum up, then drive home the truth. Illustration, inference, brief exhortation, and practical suggestion each have their place.

An elderly man thought he had found the exit from a drugstore; it was really a glass door. Three times he walked up to it and backed off because he imagined his reflection was someone else trying to get in. Shoppers watched with interest. Then the man saw his mistake and, smiling at himself in the glass, bowed and said: "Well, good morning. I'm pleased to meet you; you're looking fine." The incident ended in a chuckle. But if people can see themselves equally as well in your Bible-based sermons, it will be fine.

As an evangelistic sermon draws to a close it is logical that an invitation to come to Christ should be given. Of course, a person may respond to the gospel without another soul knowing about it at the time. But if you have been preaching for a verdict, decisions will have been made, so further help will be needed. This drawing the net in is sometimes called an altar call, an appeal, or an invitation. It is important. God draws men unto Himself; Jesus came to seek and save that which was lost, and gospel preachers are to do the same.

On the part of the hearers, a decision is inevitable. If Jesus the Saviour has been set forth in the preaching, each man must decide either to accept or reject Him. Even shelving the matter is a decision—a decision not to accept. Therefore, believing that the Holy Spirit is confirming the truth of the message by His convicting power—and while all are praying you ask for personal response to be indicated by the raising of the hand. Incidentally, this is another reason why it is best to have one aim for each message; the approach to the unsaved is different from that to the confessed Christian.

This is a momentous part of an evangelistic service. The preacher feels the awesomeness of the decisions being made. He longs that men will yield to Christ. He is filled with compassion for souls and yearns to win those who are balanced on the knife edge of decision.

He is constrained, or restrained, by the Holy Spirit as he pleads and waits. Sensitive to the leading of God, he may say few words. He wants what he does say to count. Often, God seems to put words into his mouth causing him to utter that which just fits a need, answers a question, or exposes a doubt. Here is miracle, wonder, rejoicing.

Those who have raised their hand are invited to come forward, either to the "altar" or a prayer room. This could be during the singing of an invitational hymn. Selected workers will watch for and accompany inquirers. The one-to-one contact is imperative for the Word of God must be used, both to show the foundation of salvation and the first lessons for the soul newborn. The relationship with God, finally, is individual and utterly personal.

> Just as I am, Thy love unknown
> Has broken ev'ry barrier down;
> Now to be Thine and Thine, alone,
>   O Lamb of God, I come.

Memory

There is no experience in the Christian life so full of peril as the hour when we are flushed with recent victory. Then comes the temptation to sacrifice to our net, and burn incense to our drag. We magnify our part in the conflict till it fills the whole range of vision. We boast to ourselves that we have gotten the land in possession by our own sword, and that our own arm has saved us. Counting from our great triumph at Jericho, we despise such a small obstacle as Ai. Surely, we argue, if we have carried the one, we shall easily prevail at the other. And so it frequently happens that a great success in public is followed by a fall in private; that those who had swept all before them in the pulpit or on the platform are overcome by some miserable appetite, or by petulance in the home; and the bitter regret of that sin wipes out all the glad exhilaration of the hour of victory. We never so need to observe the injunction to "watch and pray" as when the foe is flying before us.

—F. B. Meyer
Joshua and the Land of Promise

14
MEMORY

After unburdening himself of his message, a preacher can be assailed by all kinds of reactionary feelings.

First, there is a sense of relief: the burden of the message is gone. The toil and travail are over—at least for the present.

Then moments of reflection steal up on us when, to use the words of Hannah Whitall Smith, "the soul either congratulates itself upon its success and is lifted up; or it is distressed over its failure and is utterly cast down." To yield to the pressures of either of these emotional extremes is not wise. In any case, our subjective feelings are not the measure of what has been accomplished. This, for ministers especially, is an invaluable lesson to learn. "Never indulge," says an old writer, "at the close of an action in any self-reflective acts of any kind whether of self-congratulation or of self-despair. Forget the things that are behind the moment they are past, leaving them with God." We would add that later days often bring evidence that the preacher was most a blessing when least he felt it.

Another reason for learning how to control emotions is that they vitally affect our total health. W. B. Pitkin writes:

> The commonest evil result of strong emotions develops somewhere in the digestive tract. Sometimes the throat gets horribly tense. Again it is the stomach which tightens up so badly that it cannot perform the digestive movements. It may even be the colon, whose spasms bring on constipation and ulcers and appendicitis. Such disasters are never brought on by a single emotional shock that passes after a few minutes. They come only after many prolonged tensions of fear, worry, or anger have set up a habit in the muscles.[*]

The devil has a great opportunity when there is an unstable equilibrium.

The juniper tree experience is not confined to Elijah. When he gave way to numbering the faithful, depression and self-pity submerged him. He felt utterly alone and wanted to die. You too may often feel miserable because your congregation was small and evident response so slight. This is the peril of trying to measure spiritual results by human standards. On a snowy January Sunday morning, about a dozen people gathered in a Primitive Methodist Chapel. Because of impassable roads the minister couldn't make it. Everyone in the tiny congregation was known, except a fifteen-year-old boy sitting under the gallery. There were whispered consultations among the men and, at last, "a poor, thin-looking man, a shoemaker, a tailor, or something of that sort" listened to the urgings of the others and entered the pulpit.

The boy, who for some time had been deeply concerned about his sins, watched curiously as the man awkwardly ascended the pulpit stairs. His text was: "Look unto me, and be ye saved, all the ends of the earth." Whatever else was lacking, these words were just what that boy needed.

[*]W. B. Pitkin, *Take It Easy* (New York: Simon & Schuster, Inc, 1935.) Reprinted in Reader's Digest anthology, *How to Live With Life*.

He looked in faith to Jesus and found salvation in Him. Just one boy.

In that church today there is a marble tablet on the wall near the place where that fifteen-year-old sat. The inscription tells that the boy sitting under the gallery that very morning, was converted. He was only fifteen, and he died at 57. But in the intervening years he preached the gospel to millions and led thousands into the Kingdom and service of Christ. Just one boy—Charles Haddon Spurgeon.

Writing of Wesley's conversion, W. E. H. Lecky, the 19th century historian says: "The humble meeting in Aldersgate Street, London, forms an epoch in English history. It led to that great revolution (religious) in England which is of greater historic importance than all the splendid victories by land and sea won under Pitt." Just one soul. God only knows true results.

If possible, listen to recordings of your sermons after several weeks have passed. Listen critically to find the answer to questions such as these:

Did ideas develop logically?

Were points made with clarity?

How much of it was superfluous?

Was I talking too rapidly? too slowly?

Was the presentation monotonous?

What could I do to impart more life?

How would I rate this sermon if someone else preached it?

Did I close when I should? or did I hover?

Such self-criticism may not come easily, but it will do you a power of good.

As a technical detail, you may feel it wise to number each sermon so that you can index it before filing it. It is well to note where it was preached.

Elsewhere we have emphasized the value to preachers

of writing. If a man is not naturally fluent, constant writing will help to overcome this handicap. If he is naturally fluent, writing will save him from verbosity and help him to find the best words.

Your sermons, if written as articles, can reach and bless many times more people than your spoken messages. Most of the sermons used as examples in this book have been published in magazines. So why not sit down and start writing? Don't wait for the mood—life is too short. Write and the mood will come. Borrow instruction books from your library or take a writing course. You will find a greatly extended ministry through the pen.

Your first attempts may be rejected by editors, but failure is a teacher—maybe the best. Be like one enthusiast who aimed at a thousand rejection slips. Each one, he felt, taught him so much and brought him nearer to success.

You will, of course, soon discover there is a difference between the spoken word and the written word. You will come to appreciate the adage, "Brevity is the soul of wit." Think of the tremendous effect of the Communist Manifesto written by Marx and Engels. Yet it is a mere fifteen thousand words. The Declaration of Independence has less than two thousand words. "If you would be pungent, be brief," said Robert Southey. "For it is with words as with sunbeams—the more they are condensed, the deeper they burn."

Writing can become a form of recreation. It is not so for all men. But all ministers need to learn how to relax. The astonishing performance of the human heart is because of the way God has provided for its relaxation. The five or six quarts of blood in the average human body —it is said—make a round trip about once every minute. In 24 hours the heart receives and pumps out again some ten thousand quarts of blood and expends enough energy to raise a one hundred fifty pound man one thousand two hundred fifty feet in the air. In a life span of seventy years the heart lubb-dups some twenty-five hundred million times without a single shut-down for repairs. The tiny pauses between the lubb and the dup provide rest enough. The normal heart spends more than twice as much time relaxing as it does at work.

Routine has been described as God's way of saving us between our crises. We are not mounting up with wings as eagles all the time; neither are we called, always, to be running without weariness; most of our days are best described as *walking*. We can summon up enthusiasm and strength for life's high demands, but the steady claims of the everyday are more exacting. It is here we really need help. We can meet these daily duties and demands in different ways.

For example, we can look at them with indifference. This will mean we are wasting God's time and misusing the people who suupport us financially.

Or we can, like men of straw, be blown any way by the strongest breeze. We are at the mercy of the most forceful claim upon our interest, the first person who calls us or the day's most insistent demand. We have no schedule for our days so, like a man lost in a forest, we roam round in circles.

Therefore, we need to plan our days in fellowship with our Lord. Without going into details we will simply point out the priorities. There must be, as an earlier chapter has explained, the regular, early tryst with God. The rest of the morning hours should be blocked out for Bible study and sermon preparation, at least five mornings a week. Prayer and the ministry of the Word are God's first requirements of us. The fellowship thus cultivated and the practice so gained will best prepare us for God's business. The world's foremost cellist, Pablo Casals, at 89, was asked why he continued to practice four or five hours a day. "Because I think I am making progress," was the humble answer of a discerning man. Should the Lord's servant show any less dedication?

Clarence E. Macartney writes:

> A question which his friends will ask a minister who has served as long as I have, and which the minister will ask himself, is this: What would you change, do differently, if you could begin your ministry over again? What did you leave undone that you would now do, and what did you do that you would now leave undone? What different methods would you follow? If I had my ministry to commence over again, I would devote more time to prayer, meditation and the study of the Bible, although my preaching has been based entirely on the Bible. I would take more time off, too, and not run the risk to health which I have run through too long hours of work by day and by night.

This veteran's words stress devotion to priorities and attention to spiritual renewal.

There are classics of soul culture that a minister should read—slowly, prayerfully, and repeatedly. God has a way of speaking to our hearts through the written words of His choice servants. Oswald Chambers observes:

> "Knowing the terror of the Lord, we persuaide men." We can take our sanctification and our salvation too cheaply, without realizing that Jesus Christ went through deep waters of uttermost damnation that we might receive it. We read that a great fear came across the members of the early church.... They realized, what we have to realize, that the Pentecostal dispensation produces not only Pentecostal living people, but liars to the Holy Ghost.

A minister needs to ponder words like these.

Hannah Whitall Smith, the author of *The Christian's Secret of a Happy Life* remarks:

> The standard of practical holy living has been so low among Christians that the least degree of real devotedness of life and walk is looked upon with surprise and often with disapprobation, by a large portion of the Church. And, for the most part, the followers of the Lord Jesus Christ

are satisfied with a life so conformed to the world, and so like it in almost every respect, that, to a casual observer, no difference is discernable.

These are the opinions of the writer of one of the most dynamic books on Christian living.

The intrepid apostle Paul, whose illustrious life fills so much of the New Testament, tells of a fear that hung over his head, "Lest, after preaching to other people, I am disqualified myself" (1 Corinthians 9:27, Moffatt). It was not the security of his salvation in Christ that caused this fear but the possibility that his service for Christ might be found wanting. This led him to regard himself as an athlete in training. He sought to live temperately and restrict himself in all things. "I do not run uncertainly," he said, "without definite aim. I do not box as one beating the air and striking without an adversary. But [like a boxer] I buffet my body—handle it roughly, discipline it by hardships—and subdue it" (1 Corinthians 9:26, 27, Amplified). Always he kept his responsibility and accountability in view.

In certain early American Indian tribes when a princess came of age, she was given a basket and instructed to pick the best ears of corn in a given row. There was one condition—she must choose the ears as she went along. She could not turn back and select ears she had passed by. It is said that many a princess failed this test of judgment. She marvelled at the high quality of the corn and, as she felt the firm ears on the stalks, she was tempted to pick them. But perhaps there were better ears just ahead. So, while looking for perfection she missed gathering any ears at all.

For you, beginner preacher, the opportunity to prepare and practice is now.

INDEX OF PERSONS AND SUBJECTS